SAMUEL PEPYS
IN THE DIARY

PERCIVAL HUNT

SAMUEL PEPYS
IN THE DIARY

Mens cujusque is est quisque

UNIVERSITY OF PITTSBURGH PRESS

1958

© 1958

UNIVERSITY OF PITTSBURGH PRESS

Library of Congress Card Catalog Number: 58-13078

The shield on the title page is Samuel Pepys's: "sable, on a bend, or, between two nags' heads erased argent, three fleurs de lis of the field." (*See* Earl of Cottenham, *Burke's Peerage*, p. xxvii.)

PRINTED IN U. S. A.

Gratitude to

A.L.S. and B.C.S., 1958

FOREWORD

Never excuse, Shakespeare wrote. I do not know that he ever wrote, *Never explain.*

In these papers are many dates. They rain down continually. They are here because it seemed to me the time when anything was said or done gave meaning to the statement or the act, and because I hoped someone might read in the Diary what I only touched. Quotations are constant because Pepys wrote exactly and freshly, and because a quotation is firsthand authority, not just an opinion. The repetition from paper to paper comes mainly because each paper was written to be read by itself.

The explanations are personal, but—to quote again—*The purpose of the writing of this book was for my own enjoyment, to the which I was ever much inclined.* (Jean Froissart, 1333-1419.)

These papers are based on the Diary.

Percival Hunt, 1958

CONTENTS

DATES

Lord Sandwich born
May 28, 1625

Pepys born
February 23, 1633

Elizabeth Le Marchant de St. Michel born
October 23, 1640

Pepys at St. Paul's School
1643 [?] - 1650

Charles I executed
January 30, 1649

Pepys at Cambridge
March 1651-October 1653

Pepys married (Civil Ceremony, December 1)
October 10, 1655

Diary begun
January 1, 1660

The Restoration (Charles II lands at Dover)
May 25, 1660

Pepys became Clerk of the Acts
July 13, 1660

Dutch defeated
June 3, 1664

The Plague
1665

The Great Fire
September, 1666

Diary ended
May 31, 1669

Samuel Pepys: *February 23, 1663-May 26, 1703*
Elizabeth Pepys: *October 23, 1640-November 10, 1669*

SUBSTANCE IN THE DIARY

Circle and Tangents

When Pepys was thirty-eight, the wise, learned, wealthy, aristocratic, distinguished, and travelled John Evelyn wrote: "This day dined with me ... Mr. Pepys, Clerk of the Acts ... extraordinary, ingenious, and knowing." (February 19, 1671.) Thirty-two years later Evelyn wrote: "This day died Mr. Samuel Pepys," and followed that with a page of eulogy. Pepys was "a very worthy, industrious and curious person, none in England exceeding him in knowledge of the navy, ... with great integrity ... He was universally beloved, hospitable, generous, learned in many things, skilled in music, a very great cherisher of learned men." He was to be given, deservedly, "magnificent obsequies" (May 26, 1703). The eulogy was written by a scrupulous man, scanty in praise. It is a heaping up of praise by a man who knew Pepys well—all but the Diary. Still, the eulogy is not far from what Evelyn had written thirty years before, and it is not far from what the Diary shows Pepys to be.

The Diary does tell much that Evelyn did not know. It shows, on every day, the details of Pepys's life, the immediate matters in his mind, his intimate, passing, pressing views. Yet the Diary, though it tells much triviality and fault and many passionate acts and feelings and impulsive opinions and slight encounters, puts as a whole the emphasis on what Pepys held important and what caused Evelyn to write of him as he did. In the ten years of the Diary passing matters are shown to be passing; the important gets importance.

It is interesting to sort out in the long flow of the Diary what Pepys showed he thought important, day after day, in his life: to separate the sparks that fly upward and the fire that lasts. That is not easy, for ideas and moods and actions which Pepys clearly did not think important he told with a vividness that made them

1

seem important. Because of such telling, weight has been given to what he knew was slight stuff, blown into and out of his mind. An off-hand thrust of dislike felt and forgotten, some twinge of irritation or prejudice or pleasure stand out, all intense shadows or sharp brightness. Often his disgust or his admiration ("the best ever I saw in my life!") passed as it was being said. The reality faded with the expression. Indeed, in spite of the ups and downs of his impulsive moments, his scales gave fairly just weight. For example, he liked going to a play. He went at least 300 times in nine years, and he wrote of plays and knew the actors and managers and authors, but he never gave play-going the place he gave his home or his work at the Navy Office. Even his delight in people and books, alive and repeatedly expressed, makes way for what he recognized were larger. So clothes and perriwigs and Vauxhall and visiting and singing and eating, little quarrels with his wife, jealousies, his long dislike for some colleagues, his impatience with some of his relatives, his attraction toward women, fall into a background of minor worth.

Pepys's liking for women has been much written about. He did like them and said so (though not so often as he is credited with), circling in a round from his far-off but "dear Lady Castlemaine" ("Lady Castlemaine, without whom all is nothing") to the immediate housemaid. He wrote of them often. He wrote frankly, so frankly that part of it is not printed. And he wrote in a foolish mystery of mixed French and Spanish and Latin that could never deceive anyone. All this is striking, and it amuses—and it attracts much attention to a minor topic. His waywardnesses did get him into difficulties, but after his detours he came out again upon his main straight-ahead road. Casual women slipped into his life at lightly occupied or empty times. They did not turn him from what he seriously intended.

Almost every day, Pepys wrote of his wife, or if he did not write of her she is shadowed in his day's account. She was part of him. He was not always pleased with himself, and he was not always pleased with her. He worried about her, or was exasperated or angry with her as he often was with himself. The Diary gives a sense of their unity. She was to him part of himself; she was there. Often he had great satisfaction, "content," in that certainty. Often he did not. But countering all her deficiencies, she kept to the end the reality, the old lasting variety, the charm of being herself.

And in the Diary, after late 1661, he gave full importance to his work at the Navy Office. At first, the appointment was only the source of his income, a gift got by favor, a step-up through grace of Lord Sandwich. He measured it by its pay and position; and in the first month he was ready to sell his office for 1000 pounds if he "found my Lord willing to it" (August 10, 1660). The 1000 pounds "made my mouth water." Time went by and his measure of the Clerkship changed. He saw it as the power which would carry ahead his ambitions. Then toward the end, years later, he served in it because it was worth serving. He got to see that he held a position of responsibility and power for his business. His moral responsibility was to strengthen the Navy as well as he could by ships and men and supplies and administrative management. He saw that England depended on the Navy almost for existence.

Other matters beside his work and his wife were important, if less: his relations with Lord and Lady Sandwich, his duties to his often unattractive kin, London with its flowing life, his colleagues, his household, all that was curious and new, some of his friendships, and the Diary.

Pepys wrote a great deal about his quiet relations with people whom he liked—with his clerks, the Hunts, Lady Sandwich and her children, the Crews, John Evelyn, his cousin Jane Turner and her very young daughter, and others; most of all and strongest with Will Hewer. Not much comment has been made on these entries. They are not dramatic bursts and are not often picturesque, yet all through the Diary they stand solidly part of it. Possibly they show as truly the weight of his qualities and character as more exciting entries show.

His clerks were, he said, his "other family," and he kept them in his mind. Mr. and Mrs. Hunt had been his good neighbors when he was just married and was living "very poor" in his garret. He names them close to a hundred times, hardly ever without praising them. They are, when the Diary ends, "as good people as I hardly know any," "people I do love." Lady Sandwich, he honored and liked to be with and he served her well from first to last. His kind, gay, sensible, rich religious cousin, Mrs. Jane Turner, was the wife of John Turner, sergeant-at-law and a Templar. They lived in the quiet of Salisbury Court, close to his father's shop. She took Pepys into her comfortable house when he was cut for the stone in 1658. They stayed good friends.

Will Hewer came into the Diary the first night Pepys ever lay in his house in Seething Lane. When he went home late that night he found his wife gone to bed, Jane still washing the woodwork, "Will the boy sleeping: and . . . great deal of sport I had before

3

I could wake him." Will Hewer then was part clerk and part personal servant to Pepys, and lived in Pepys's house. He was 18. His pay in money was 30 pounds a year; Pepys at first kept part of it. Pepys liked Will: he "is so obedient, that I am greatly glad of him" (July 17, 1660), yet he had faults. At times he kept his hat on in the house before his master and mistress—"a proud trick," seeming to show "his pride and laziness ... though in other things he is good enough." He proved more than good enough. Twenty-eight years after he came to Pepys, when he was secure and wealthy and Pepys was out of office and in danger, he wrote to Pepys: "all I have proceeded from you; so all I have and am, is and shall be at your service" (December 16, 1688). Pepys endorsed the letter: "a letter of great kindness at a time of difficulty." He and Pepys were living together in Clapham when Pepys died. My "most approved and most dear friend William Hewer of Clapham, in the County of Surry, Esquire," Pepys names him in his will.

The Diary was important. Monday of the Great Fire he took it to safety at Bethnal Green, and he carried it home among what he first returned. He ended the Diary when he thought he was going blind. The last paragraph he wrote in it is: "And so I betake myself to that course [ending the Diary], which is almost as much as to see myself go into my grave: for which, and all the discomforts that will accompany my being blind, the good God prepare me! S.P. May 31, 1666."

Topics

Pepys wrote of his daily affairs. He did not write for the future, or to show wonders and himself to lesser people, or, it seems, even for his own rereading. He wrote a chronicle day by day, a log of his actions, thoughts, and feelings, a direct account of his life, with not many sweeps of philosophy or abstraction. He did philosophize but not usually. He philosophized on his having got his position by favor, on the need that words of a song be left in the language in which they were written, on his lack of lasting sorrow when his brother died, on the conduct of the King and Court ("God knows what will be the end of it!"), on London after the Fire and after the Plague. He wrote of his childhood at Ashted when he went back there at thirty; and he wrote a tremendously effective and self-forgetful account of the Fire. But philosophizing is not the main recurring substance of the Diary; it is in the Diary because it was part of some day in his life.

Pepys had the luck or the instinct or the determination to be in important places at important times, often in places he has no busi-

4

ness to be. Once there, he shoved his way, quite unashamed, to the front. Possibly what he wrote made up for his elbowing. At sixteen he stood close by the scaffold when Charles I was beheaded on a cold January afternoon; and at twenty-six, time having changed his fortune and opinion, he went to see General Harrison, who had signed the King's death-warrant, hanged and drawn and quartered —"a bloody day." He was in London when Oliver Cromwell died; and when Richard Cromwell gave up his ineffectual rule; and while Parliament and the Army struggled; and he watched, one morning in February, 1660, "it being a most pleasant morning and sunshine," General Monk march his men into control of the City ("all his forces . . . in very good plight and stout officers"). He was secretary to the Admiral on the "Royal Charles," which brought Charles II back to England, and he saw him land at Dover and ride away to London "in a stately coach." At the coronation he pushed into the Abbey among the followers of the King's Surveyor-General and from a seat high up under the roof of the North Transept he saw and heard what he could. (At the next coronation, as a baron of the Cinque Ports, he walked close by the King.) When the new Queen (September 21, 1662), whom everybody was curious about, heard her first mass in her Chapel of St. James's, he crowded close up to the altar and to the Queen; and since his cousin was the ambassador and admiral whose ship carried the Queen from Portugal, Pepys heard much about her. He was in London during the Plague, and he watched almost hour by hour the Great Fire. He knew the King, the Duke of York, the Court, and some of the King's ladies. He saw the Established Church return with the Restoration, and the playhouses open, and the old ways come in again, though changed. He had part in the humiliations and triumphs of the endless, intermittent, vital Dutch Wars, and he lived a long time shadowed by the Popish Plot and by Titus Oates and his like. He had part in the coronation of James II, and four years after that he saw James deposed and William III come. He knew London intimately, places and people, and the quiet English country beyond, and the villages, and the farmlands. He was familiar with working-men in the City, and the men who kept the little shops and taverns, and their clerks, and the great merchants, and the banker-goldsmiths. He had been at Cambridge with Dryden; for years he talked and often ate with Thomas Fuller of the *Worthies;* he became a friend of "that miracle of a youth Christopher Wren" and of the noble Mr. John Evelyn, and of many such; and he corresponded with Sir Isaac Newton, Sir Hans Sloane, Sir Godfrey

5

Kneller, the Duchess of Newcastle, the Duke of York, and masters and dons at Oxford and Cambridge, and other learned and humane men. Most of them he wrote of in the Diary.

Details

Pepys had unending curiosity, like many others of his time. The seventeenth century and part of the eighteenth was the last age of universal, unspecialized interests. No harsh barriers were set between the arts, or between the humane and the practical. Ability practiced over wide fields. Christopher Wren was professor of astronomy at Oxford, and he built St. Paul's Cathedral. Vanbrugh wrote plays and was a great architect. Davenant was a playwright and an army colonel. Denham was the King's surveyor-general and the author of *Cooper's Hill.* Fairfax, the best English commander-in-chief for a 100 years, gave up his command because his conscience was against the Scottish Wars. John Evelyn, whom Pepys from the first judged "excellent humoured . . . and mighty knowing," was a humanist, yet he was Commissioner for the Privy Seal, for the Care of the Sick and Wounded in the Dutch War, for rebuilding St. Paul's, for governing the English Colonies, and for many other practical matters; and he worked to get the water and the air of London purified, to increase the salaries of college professors, to better the paving of some city streets which were, he said, "a quagmire." Pepys himself, who "stood in such strange slavery to beauty that [he] value[d] nothing near it," and who was sometimes petty and petulant and illogical and quite unfair, was yet clear-headed, logical, hard-working, and came to see what the Navy meant to England and fought to build it up.

His curiosity was constant and wide. It touched all manner of things, big or little, grotesque or beautiful, scientific or folk-stuff. Evelyn was delighted by what he called "the incomparable history of the silkworm"; Christopher Wren at Oxford—"that very sweet place," Pepys called it—cherished "a piece of white marble, which he had stained with a lively red, very deep, as beautiful," Evelyn wrote "as if it had been natural"; the Bishop of Chester had hives of glass for his bees "built like castles and palaces," transparent, and "adorned with a variety of dials, little statues, vanes, &c.," which Charles II went to see "and contemplate[d] with much satisfaction." The fourteenth century bestiary told as truth that the unicorn visited royally the court of the Chinese emperor, and that in Ethiopia the phoenix burned itself each year to ashes and was

6

renewed, and Phisiologus said truly that mermaids "singen wel and merily," and horsehairs left in water, did become snakes. Even to statements like these Pepys would listen, interested if not believing.

Indeed, Pepys stopped before most things new to him and gave them a look of attention. For some, one attentive moment was enough. A Royal Society lecture about "the trade of felt-making" was "very pretty" but an hour or so of it satisfied. Other matters he gave attention to according to their merit and his preference even though they were not close to him—heraldry, for instance, and law, and theology, and the history and process of coining money. Most oddities did not keep him long, though he took time to write of holding in his arms a "boy 4 years old of a prodigious bigness, about as big as a man," of a statue that spoke ("an ingenuity") of "King Henry's chair where he that sits down is catched with two irons, that come round about him, and make good sport."

He was interested by ingenious machanisms. He "admired" a "wooden jack" (a machine turning a spit to roast meat) Mr. Spong had made, which was whirled by the draft of the open fireplace (October 23, 1660). Mr. Spong was a quiet friend of his, a legal copyist, "plain and illiterate" but "ingenuous," and he played and sang, and liked to talk of music. He told Pepys "among other fine thing . . . that by his microscope of his owne making he do discover that the wings of a moth is made just as the feathers of the wing of a bird, and that most plainly and certainly" (August 7, 1664). Pepys was "mightily pleased with his company."

A new and usable instrument held him. Anthony Deane, in 1665 assistant shipwright of Woolwich (later Sir Anthony, M.P., a great shipbuilder), showed him "the use of a little sliding ruler" which Pepys had not seen before—"more portable" (May 5). Pepys thought Deane "an ingenious fellow." Wisps of curious fact he had been told or had read caught in his mind. When he dined at Trinity House (May 6, 1663), "among other discourse worth hearing . . . the old seamen, they tell us that they have catched often in Greenland . . . wales" from some of which "they have had eleven hogshead of oyle out of the tongue." And when the Matted Gallery at Whitehall was being rebuilt, he thought it "strange to see what hard matter the plaster of Paris is, as hard as stone." In some parts of Italy, he heard, snakes left their holes and gathered to be caught when a cello was played. He did not believe all he heard but he could speculate or at least collect with interest these more than doubtful travellers' tales.

His collecting of odd items was not limited by his taste or their value or by anything but his curiosity. Purple was "prince's mourning," he learned when Charles II wore it after the death of his brother, Henry, Duke of Gloucester (September 13, 1663). Doctor Williams, Elizabeth Pepys's doctor, did carry me into his garden, where he hath abundance of grapes; and did show how a dog that he hath do kill all cats that come thither to kill his pigeons, and do afterword bury them, and do it with so much care . . . that if but the tip of the tail hangs out he will take up the cat again and dig the hole deeper. Which is very strange" (September 11, 1661). Pepys learned from Captain John Stokes of the Navy, who had been to Africa, that "the country of Gambo is. . . .unhealthy, yet . . . the present King there is a hundred and fifty years old; . . . the kings there have above 100 wives apiece" (January 16, 1662). Sir Robert Viner, a rich merchant and Lord Mayor of London in 1674, showed him "a black boy that he had, that died of a consumption, and being dead, he caused him to be dried in an oven, and lies there entire in a box" (September 7, 1665). Mr. Benjamin Templer (a rector in Northamptonshire, "a person of honour he seemed to be") discoursing of the nature of serpents, told "that in the waste places of Lancashire [they] do grow to a great bigness, and . . . do feed upon larks . . . :—They observe when the lark is soared to the highest, and do crawl . . . just underneath them; and there they place themselves with their mouths uppermost, and . . . do eject poyson up to the bird; [and] the bird . . . falls directly into the mouth of the serpent; which is very strange." Mr. Templer, Pepys added, perfectly, is a great traveller" (February 4, 1662).

Once when he was thirty-four, he went to bed "vexed at two or three things, viz.: that my wife's watch proves so bad as it do; the ill state of the office; and Kingdom's business; at the charge which my mother's death for mourning will bring me when all paid." Surely things less equal in importance and kind seldom were thrown into one sentence.

He was always alertly interested in meetings of the Royal Society, to which he was elected in 1665. Two weeks after his admission, on February 15, he listened, March 1, to a "very curious lecture about the late Comett" and to "Mr. Evelyn's paper, entitled 'Panificium' . . . a very particular account of the making of the several sorts of bread in France, which is accounted the best place for bread in the world." On March 15, the legendary poison of the Upas tree, the "great poyson of Maccassa was tried upon a dogg, but it had no effect all the time we sat there." At the same meeting

8

Pepys himself reported "information he had received" from the master of an African ship "concerning the pendulum watches." A year and a half later there was an experiment in blood transfusion: "a pretty experiment of the blood of one dogg let out, till he died, into the body of another, on one side, while all his own ran out on the other side." The *History of the Royal Society* tells this was done "upon a little mastiff and a spaniel with very great success, the former bleeding to death, and the latter receiving the blood of the other" (November 14, 1666). Two weeks after, "they had good discourse how this late experiment of the dog, which is in perfect good health, may be improved for good uses to men." In the Diary, the record of many papers and many experiments runs on, always fresh and unwearying to Pepys.

Fortunately, his interests in the Navy never lost tang for him, and freshness, and fortunately his pleasure in learning and his power to learn went ahead equally with his need to learn. Even in his latest years as Clerk, he had new questions to answer. Had he, after all, found the right design for a frigate? Were New England pines best for ship masts; better than Scotch or Scandinavian or English? How could he get good chaplains and good pursers and good captains for the fleet? How could he ever find money to build ships and pay the seamen? And—the great question—where were men honest enough for him to trust, and able enough to build a good ship, and wise enough to judge truly other men?

The details of his office work had romance in them. Ships demanded (or, unchanging, waited to be given) strange and heterogeneous, almost magic sounding, supplies, about which the Clerk of the Acts must learn. Ships needed sisal and oakum and hollystone, tar, tarbuckets, braziers, hamaccos, deales, cooking pots and pans, scarlet waiste-cloathes and silken pendants, lard and tallow and much other grease, bells and capstans and marlin spikes, calico and bunting, great stores of medicines and foods, sails and cordage and spars, iron for anchors, at times trumpets and "a set of fiddles," cannons and other firearms, drums and flags and hammocks, pammican, pipeclay, pennons, banners, and a whole dictionary-long list of other sea items. All these and many more Pepys learned about with happiness and much drudgery. His colleagues and his own ignorance did at times irritate him; the strangeness of new things did baffle him for awhile; but what he was doing he found worth doing, and exciting, and satisfying. He was not compelled to learn by his office in the Navy. He liked finding out what he had to do and how to do it. He was stirred

9

with wonder. His need to know fell in with his liking to learn. It all quite suited his scientific, inclusive, childlike, and never-satisfied curiosity.

The Core of the Diary

So, year after year, line by line, Pepys went on through 1,400,000 words telling what interested him; and the number and range and variety of his comments keep unending freshness. Such freshness makes good reading, for it carries the reader along in its reality. It has great value and charm.

But it has dangers. Sometimes Pepys makes so alive a detail of no importance a reader forgets that details are not the whole of the Diary; that the flash from a page should blend into the unity of the Diary. Pepys did write trivia so brilliantly that they seem important. The little seems large. A small-part actor steps too far forward. The wording of a minor matter cuts unfairly into a reader's attention and memory and gets the stamp of importance. At the end of a busy day, for instance, Pepys wrote, "I went by link home [by lighted torch: "link-light" he sometimes calls it] ... where I found the house in a washing pickle." The last words exactly catch his feeling and the degree of it. The point is, the cleaning did seem large and possessive to him as he wrote.

Yet for all that, his details are not the core of the Diary. The core of the Diary, whether Pepys knew it or not, was the whole truth; and truth-telling needs besides brilliant reality of details the emphasis which adds up details to the right total. Pepys was unendingly interested by his own experiences and by what went on around him. Often in the Diary he is so absorbed into what he is writing, so intensely lost and centered in it, that the moment he is telling gets to have for him no time before or after. It is a moment isolated and absolute. Pepys did not, of course, mean it was isolated. He did not think that each moment was equal to each other moment, or that it was separated from it. Life was one lasting, moving activity, with infinitely differing emphasis on its infinite parts. Pepys had his main interests, his highest ratings. Even before he went to Cambridge he knew there were some things he wanted because they were in themselves important—at least to him. He never could get all he wanted. At twenty, he knew that. Yet he was sure even then that he had ability to get much he wanted; and that to live was exciting and sober. He knew he would have to work, every day, steadily and hard, toward a few ends, and that by and large he would enjoy the hard work. He did go on toward the ends

10

he had set; and the Diary shows how far he went in ten years. He worked, and he enjoyed his work and much else, and he got far ahead of anything he could have hoped for when he was twenty-six. Once in awhile to him his life was open, golden, incredible; and once in awhile he felt that he and the times were insecure, sick, more than half evil, and that he needed to turn from his ways and repent and be forgiven.

It is true that because it was his nature to be absorbed by what was happening, he gave space to feelings and acts and ideas not worth his time (though it is hard to say what is worth someone's time) and wrote crude vulgarities of gossip and spite. Yet he usually kept in clearer air. Intensity and curiosity were part of the focus of his nature, part of the animating and explanatory center of his life—for good and bad. His writing is himself. It is unified and bounded by what he was. He was one person, though more complex and more expressive than those around him. Most of the trivial matters he wrote of had no hold on him except for a moment and by their newness. They came into his sight, glowed, and were gone. He wrote of them only once. They entertained him. He might speculate about them. But they stayed unimportant and, so, unexplored. They lay on the misty rim of reality, where the pygmies and the hyperborians were and the ocean ended. In its total, the Diary shows the solid world Pepys lived in and valued immensely: a world that held his wife and his career, the English Navy, Lord and Lady Sandwich, and—less strong and mixing in and out among the others—music, books, eating, playgoing, women, and his vagrant and far-wandering curiosity, and much else.

About serious concerns, Pepys wrote increasingly and with increasing interest and maturity. What was merely strange gets less space as the Diary goes on. And it is probably fair to say that even at first most details, certainly most repeated details, are centered in the real interests of his life.

The core of the Diary is the personality of Pepys. Take, for instance, one trait and watch its expression and emphasis in the Diary.

Pepys was the best company in the world. He was interesting and interested and vibrant and sweet, and tactful because he was sensitive. All sorts of people liked him, so they were not spoiled by meanness, brutality, unfounded pride, small suspicions, and the certainty of superiority. (All these sins, Pepys showed at his worst.) And Pepys liked people. He had plenty in his mind to keep him awake when he was alone, yet people were to him a great reality on any day. If he could help it he did not eat by himself. It took away his appetite for food and for living.

Learned persons were his friends—Wren, Evelyn, Dr. Charlett of University College, Oxford, Fuller of the *Worthies*. They were intimates of his mind and his interests. They enjoyed his companionship in their way. Those who were young and those dependent on him, the intimates of his ordinary life—Will Hewer at twenty-five, his very young cousin Betty Turner, his clerks, his servants—enjoyed in quite another way another kind of companionship with him. Gentle and ingenious Mr. Spong the law scrivner, Mrs. Knipp and Lady Sandwich, Lord Crew, Mrs. Turner of the Navy Office (a waste of one's time), Jane of Axe Yard, Deb (unfortunately), and hundreds besides were happy in his company, not because of his knowledge and ability, though no doubt it touched them, but for what he was himself. Old and young, simple and learned, men and women, rank and no-rank, felt his attraction.

Not everyone, of course, liked him. To some he was a pompous, pushing, little, vulgar man. Those were mostly jealous of him and opposed to him and thought he had what he never should have had. They were mostly those shut in their self-conceit and not willing to explore.

Pepys liked being liked. To anyone who disliked or opposed him, he could give wide grounds for dislike. He had in him cutting strength and acid, small-spirited meannesses; and he had no humility or grace before what he thought was aggression.

He had courage, and more and more he grew to be his best at a crisis and in front of large matters. A small matter tempted him to be small. He had shrewdness which could rise into wisdom, tenacity that lasted out a long race, and at his best his intelligence was clear enough to prefer goodness to itself.

These and other strong qualities of Pepys are the core of the Diary.

PEPYS'S DAY

The outline of Pepys's day was set by the customs of his time. Usually, he got up at sunrise. In spring and summer and the brighter fall, sunrise meant four or five o'clock. On June 13, 1662, two years settled in his Clerkship, he was "Up by 4 o'clock in the morning, and read *Cicero's Second Oration* against *Cateline,* which pleased me exceedingly"; and ten or twelve other entries that month show he was up at four. Habit sent him, next, to business at his office, but one June morning he and Will Hewer walked by the river, and once he "took and played upon [his] lute a little," and once he again read "a little . . . Cicero." In July he worked a dark hour or two at his office, then "home, it being sunrise." Other entries for July that year run: "Up at 4 o'clock, and at my multiplication table hard" (As Clerk, he needed the tables, and had never learned them before, and found them stubborn); "Up at four and to my office"; "Up while the chimes went four and to put down my journal." A year later he went "to bed about 10 o'clock," very early for him, but the next morning "Up before 4 o'clock, which is the hour I intend now to rise at." One day in April that year, after going "betimes" to his office steadily for three weeks, he was "Up betimes, and to my vyall and song book a pretty while" before he went to his office and "there sat all the morning" (April 25, 1663). In late May, 1663: "waked this morning between four and five by my blackbird, which whistles as well as ever I heard any; only it is the beginning of many tunes very well, but there leaves them, and goes no further." So, the summer entries of time go on in 1662 and 1663; and so they do in 1664 and after.

When the fall came, he still was "Up betimes, but now the days begin to shorten, and so whereas I used to rise by four o'clock, it is not broad daylight now until after five o'clock, so that it is after five before I do rise." He was "Up by break of day at 5 o'clock" (September 5, 1662); at times he "Lay long . . . till 6 and past" (September 6); but the Diary shows he kept to his timing through most of the cold months that year and later, in 1667 and 1668. Now and then he was not out of bed until seven or eight o'clock, "it being horrid cold." Generally, on even the coldest days, he got up "by candle light about 6 o'clock, though it was bitter cold weather again" (February 27, 1667). Evil weather kept him once in bed till 11—an unusual and unseemly lapse, for which he was sorry. Such "habit we have got into this winter!" The next week he was up before light. He did stay close to what he had promised himself.

As the Diary went on Pepys less often gave exact hours; he wrote he was up betimes or very betimes or pretty betimes or early. This is like his less and less itemizing food and other unsuggesting facts as the Diary continues.

The early start of the day had roots in religion and custom and need and law. The canonical hours for prayers were set—Matins, the first hour, originally at midnight; Lauds, at sunrise; Prime, at six; Terce, nine; Sext, noon; Vespers, sunset; and Compline, nine. From the sixth century, the Great Gabriel Bell, the Angelus, rang at six, daybreak. The Bell rang its nine beats, three groups of three, so that all hearing it might "say one *Paternoster* and greet our Lady with the *Five Hail Mary's.*" The Angelus came again at twelve noon and again at six at night. Church bells went on ringing through the day. A man in the city or country counted on their soundings to tell him the hour. Englishmen were accustomed to their bells as they were to the shift of the clouds or the changes of sunlight.

The law in many towns forbade work before 4 o'clock in summer and 5 in winter, by "Knockking, fyling," and other "noysefulle werk." Most work began at six. City markets opened then; and first comers got the best; and, anyway no one ate till nine or even ten, after churchgoing and marketing. Work woke many but pleasure woke the few. Charles II in London at six played tennis; Lord Chief Justice Coke began working at three; Henry VIII's Queen Katherine of Aragon was dressed for the day at five; and *A Midsummer Night's Dream* tells, Duke Theseus in Athens had been out before daylight with his hounds. Pepys was up by five or six. Elizabeth Pepys woke as early as he. In May, Pepys once was "Troubled, about three in the morning, with [his] wife's calling her maid up, and rising herself, to go with her coach abroad, to gather May-dew," incomparable for beauty. The next day she was up at 4, to go again for May-dew (1669).

The seventeenth century ate no breakfast. A laborer might or might not have bread and beer, but, said a foreign visitor, "how-

14

soever those that journey and some sickly men staying at home may perhaps take a small breakfast, yet in general the English eat it not." Pepys spent the first hour or so dressing, talking, studying, at his music, writing in the Diary, practicing "some arithmetique," listening as his wife read to him, or he went straight to his office.

About 8:00 he began business appointments outside his office, and at 9:30 he had what was his breakfast and then stayed in his office until he went to dinner at half-past twelve. Breakfast was usually only mid-morning ale at a tavern. "Into an ale-house and drank," he wrote; had "a pint of wine"; took a "morning draft at the Samson in Paul's Church-yard," or "burnt wine at the Rose Tavern," or stopped at "the Swan for morning draft," or "at the Sun" for "a morning draft of Muscadine." Once he drank "a cold small beer . . . in a cold room." Tea and coffee and chocolate were not common until at least fifty years later. Pepys had his first cup of tea, a novelty for England, in 1660. Unfortunately he made no comment about it. Six years later Elizabeth Pepys was drinking tea as a medicine; "Mr. Pelling, the Potticary, tells her it is good for her cold and defluxions" (June 28, 1667). In a friend's garden, he had "wine and fruit from a tree"; in the country, "beer and a dish of eggs"; and rarely he tells of a cut of brawn, some pickled herrings, oysters, or the like. Mostly, the pint made the breakfast.

Dinner was the main meal of the day. It was eaten at noon. Pepys had his dinner at home; his office and home were in the same building, a door between. One leisurely Sunday morning, he went "round about by the street to my office." (September 7, 1662). A century earlier, in Shakespeare's time, dinner was at eleven or half-past eleven; a century before that, in the fifteenth century, it came at ten or half-past, and in the fourteenth, at nine or just after.

Pepys and his wife ate simply. In their less ample days, they might for dinner have a calf's head with bacon or with dumplings, or "nothing but a dish of the left-over turkey" (. . . "which my wife dressed and burned her hand at" . . .). They might have "a cut of brawn with cabbage," "a dish of steak and rabbits," mutton-pie, "cod's-head," "poor Jack" (low-grade codfish), a "Dish of Soles & Flounders with Crab Sauce," "Liver Fryde." One day he ate only peas-porridge, another day had only bread and cheese and a cup of ale, but on a third he had "an excellent dish of tripe covered with mustard," a dish he had seen at Lord Crew's. With his wife he enjoyed, "a good hog's harslet [heart, liver, etc.], a piece of meat

15

I love, but have not eat of I think these seven years." He had "collared eel" [wound in a coil]; and once, four months in office, "some hog's pudding of my Lady's making, of the hog that I saw a fattening the other day at her house"; and once "creame and brown bread," which he enjoyed very much (July 13, 1665).

The variety and level of their food rose in the 1660's with their rising income. They dined then on "rost beef," or a good piece of "powdered beef" [beef sprinkled with salt], or a "powdered" leg of pork or of lamb. They had in the late 1660's "fine salmon pie," "good ribs of beef and mince pies and plenty of good wine," and at Bristol "strawberries, a whole venison-pastry, cold, and plenty of . . . wine, and above all Bristoll milk" [sherry]. Pepys in one entry was proud that he and his wife had at noon "a good venison pastry and a turkey to ourselves, without anybody so much as invited by us, a thing unusual for so small a family of my condition" (January 1, 1665). Meat was the center of dinner. Part of the year, it needed to be kept in brine or "powdered with salt" or served with high spicing. Pepys wrote for June 30, 1668, as not unusual: "then home for dinner, where a stinking leg of mutton, the weather being very wet and hot to keep meat in." He wrote of pastries and pudding, and tarts, and spiced buns very sweet, and a "stately cake," all which food both he and his wife liked. Meat, if part of the meal, is always mentioned. Ale or beer might be, wine usually was; but bread and butter and milk and common fruit and common vegetables and common herbs seem taken for granted. In London, all sorts of berries could be bought and a surprising abundance and variety of fruits—apples, pears, peaches, quinces, strawberries, nectarines, figs, oranges, lemons, musk-mellons (at five or six shillings), hot-house grapes and common grapes, and even pomengrantes. Pineapples were for the King.

Afternoon blended into evening. No meal divided them. Pepys did not "sup" until just before he went to his prayers and to bed, and then lightly. Supper, like breakfast, was not formal. It was a matter, perhaps, of "bread and cheese and ale," or of "curds and cream," or with a guest of "mince pie and wine and the remnant of my collar of brawn," or "a good supper, part of my dinner today" (September 20, 1668), or it was a bit of bread and butter," a flagon of ale and apples, drunk out of a wooden cup," and, in Lent, sometimes "wiggs [tea-cakes or buns] and ale" (April 8, 1664). At Sir William Penn's once for supper it was "butter and radishes" (May 17, 1667)—strange companions. In the 1600's radishes were held in great honor for the body. Radishes "procure appetite and help

16

dygestion" (1655); and Pepys on shipboard had "In the morning ... a breakfast of radishes at the Purser's table" (May 2, 1660).

In his early thirties, Pepys found that for his health he must lay "aside that practice of eating late and of irregular eating" at night. So he lessened his suppers. But one evening, when he was twenty-seven, at the Hoop Tavern "by the Bridge," he and three others "drank off two or three quarts of wine, which was very good; ... and we did eat above 200 walnuts." His feeling the next day strengthened his value for abstinence: "To-day not well of my last night's drinking yet." A suitable uneasy-sounding sentence.

So the outline of the day was set: up at daylight; morning work and mid-morning draught; dinner at half-past twelve; the variety of afternoon and evening; supper, prayers, and bed.

* * * * * *

Pepys, as he wrote again and again, was troubled because he sat up later than he should. In 1660 he "never supped or very seldom before 12 at night." He kept at his Diary "till the bell-man came by with his bell just under my window as I was writing this very line, and cried, 'Past One of the clock, and a cold, frosty, windy morning'"; and in June he walked in his garden till twelve, and often till twelve worked at his office. A year after that he still regretted "being found a-bed aday by all sorts of people" because of his "trick of sitting up later than he need." He tells of his once supping early. It was February. He walked "in the garden by brave moonlight with [his] wife, above two hours, till past 8 o'clock, then to supper."

The small amount of food Pepys ate is a surprise. Often come such entries as these: "ate nothing but a bit of cheese today"; "nothing but a dish of sheep's trotters"; "at the Dog Tavern ... a dish of anchovies [which he had fairly often] and olives"; had only "a little supper"; "had only some porridge." On the anxious, occupied day he got his patent sealed as Clerk of the Acts (July 13, 1660), he ate "nothing but a bit of bread and cheese at Lilly's ... and a bit of bread and butter after I was a-bed." That night he went to "bed with the greatest quiet of mind I have had a great while."

Very often when Elizabeth Pepys was not well Pepys "dined by her bedside." He liked this being with her; and besides he liked company and never was happy to eat alone. Christmas Day, 1662, he wrote "I walked home again with great pleasure, and there dined by my wife's bed-side with great content, having a mess of

17

brave plum-porridge and a rosted pullet for dinner, and I sent for a mince-pie abroad, my wife not being well to make any herself yet."

As the Diary goes on, Pepys itemizes food less and less, probably because his ability to buy fine food less and less dazzled him. It did not any longer measure success. Yet, to the end of the Diary he displays his thirty fine silver dishes. Even in his sharp summary of England's distress written after the Great Fire, he said, "One thing I reckon remarkable in my owne condition is, that I am come to abound in good plate, so as at all entertainments to be served wholey with silver plates, having two dozen and a half." This is his ending and typical sentence for the year 1666.

From first to last, two things went "much against [his] stomach": dirty hands at cooking and a dirty dish—greasy, finger-marked, filmed. At his Aunt Wight's (January 1, 1664) the sight of her hands made a hot swan pie so uneatable that he and his wife "rose from the table, pretending business, and went to the Duke's house" (to *Henry VIII*). He did not like the play. At a supper with Sir William Penn "the dishes were so deadly foule that I could not endure to look upon them" (January 17, 1664). He and his wife had dinner, in September, 1667, at Mrs. Pierce's, "the nastiest poor dinner that made me sick!" Besides, Mrs. Pierce was "painted which made me loathe her." (Evelyn had found painting "a most ignominious thing, and used only by prostitutes.") "Being tired of being here, and sick of their damned slutish dinner," Pepys and his wife went to the play. At the table of the great Lord Albemarle ("a dull heavy man") and his Duchess ("ever a plain homely dowdy and worse") he had "an ill dinner," mainly from "dirty dishes" (April 4, 1667). He was scrupulous about food and service and such matters in his house. Elizabeth Pepys learned to meet exacting demands on her house-keeping.

* * * * * *

Music was a constant part of his day. In the early morning, before he went to his office, he often played or sang or listened to the playing of others. There was music at the tavern as he took his ale. Afternoon visiting or going to the play brought music, and the evening might begin and continue and end with it. Many of his friends were professional musicians; most of the people he lived among, from the King to his wife's maid, sang or played or at least liked music.

Music was everywhere in England—at the Court, in churches and cathedrals, in taverns and homes, and in the houses of the

18

great and on village greens. All over England was music, music native or foreign—sung by Englishmen and played on English fiddles and brasses, and on English organs and bells and drums and lutes; or set by foreign taste to strange cadences and strange instruments.

A PRINCIPAL OFFICER

"... thou art translated."

On the first of May, 1660, the Commons restored "Government of King, Lords and Commons," and, standing, with heads uncovered, they asked Charles to come back as their King. The next day Pepys, who was with the Channel Fleet, secretary to Sir Edward Montague, the Admiral, wrote: "Great joy all yesterday in London, and at night more bonfires than ever, and ringing of bells, and drinking of the King's health upon their knees in the streets, which methinks is a little too much." In London, Charles was formally proclaimed King on May 8, with trumpets and heralds and full ceremony; on the thirteenth the Fleet sailed for Holland to bring him home; and on the twenty-fifth he landed at Dover and entered into his kingdom.

Charles II rewarded many who had stood by his father and him, and forgot much light disloyalty. He made Sir Edward Montague, Pepys's second cousin and patron, an earl and gave him the Garter, and he promised Sir Edward that Pepys should be Clerk of the Acts. To have the promise seemed a miracle to Pepys, though he did not know just what Clerk of the Acts was except that it was a well-paid office and high in the Admiralty. He was grateful to Sir Edward.

All through the early summer of 1660 Pepys stood in doubt of being appointed. Other men backed by great influences wanted the place. June 29 he had his "warrant from the Duke [of York, Head of the Admiralty] to be Clerk of the Acts," but it was not signed by the King. Pepys waited. Then, as the official appointment hung day after day uncertain, he set to work in "a dispair" to end the uncertainty. July 10 he "put on [his] new silk suit, the first that ever I wore in my life," and went to the Attorney General's, and got his bill, his unsigned warrant of office, and the same day persuaded Lord Sandwich "to go to the Secretary's ... and desire the dispatch of his, and my bills to be signed by the King. . . . Home, with my mind pretty quiet." July 11, he had his bill back, signed by the King. To become Clerk he needed, after he had made some preliminary office-visits, only to have the warrant engrossed—written out in legal handwriting—and sealed with the Lord Chancellor's seal. Pepys again set to work. He had difficulties. The afternoon and evening of the twelfth he "was forced to run all up and down Chancery-lane . . . but could find none that could write the [legal] hand, that were at leisure." At eleven that night he did come upon an old friend, Mr. Spong the scrivener, and "got him . . . to take my bill to write it himself (which was a great providence . . .) against tomorrow morning." Even late that night he was "In great trouble," for he heard that a rival for the place had "said that he would make a stop in the business."

By eight the next morning, July 13, Pepys was at Mr. Spong's. He found him "in his night-gown writing of my patent." Mr. Spong finished the engrossing and Pepys at once "carried it . . . to the Chancellor's," got a "recept" for it, took it to another office "for a dockett" and left it after giving the clerk of the office "two pieces" —a little less than ten shillings. The rest of the morning, Pepys spent his time and his money in other offices, "much troubled in mind about my patent . . . for fear of another change." At noon, by chance he met Mr. Spong in the street and was glad to see him, and at Lilly's tavern they "ate some bread and cheese" and drank together. Next, he went home, got more money (office visiting was expensive), and brought his wife with him by coach into London. He left her in the coach, waiting, and went again to the Lord Chancellor's. There, "beyond all expectation," he was given his patent with the seal at last on it. He was Clerk of the Acts. With the patent, Pepys as he tells it, "went to my wife again, whom I had left in a coach at the door of Hinde Court, and presented her with my patent at which she was overjoyed; so to the Navy office, and showed her my house and were both mightily pleased at all things there." Two days later he writes again: "My wife and I mightily pleased with our new house. . . . My patent has cost me a great deal of money, about £40, which is the only thing at present which do trouble me much" (July 15).

Besides a salary of 380 pounds a year, the appointment carried with it fees and what Pepys calls a "house," a part of the Navy Office Building. The Navy Office was in a large space at the southeast corner of Seething Lane and Hart Street, opposite St. Olave's church, with entrance from each of those streets. It had courtyards

21

and spreading wings and gardens, and part of it was four or five stories high. In the great building, the "principal Officers of the Navy" (Pepys's description) had their offices and might live if they wished. Pepys liked the new house. It was a gentleman's house, dignified, large, and well-designed. He had a garden, cellars, a "below stairs," a main floor, and a floor above the main one. Later, 1662, he added a storey. Over part of it at least was a flat roof, "the leads," where he walked and rested and sang, and much enjoyed himself.

"... great ones of the city"

In the Pepys Library is a list, written by Pepys, of the Admiralty Officers, May 31, 1660.

His Royal Highness James, Duke of York, Lord High Admiral.
Sir George Carteret, Treasurer.
Sir Robert Slingsby, [soon after] Comptroller.
Sir William Batten, Surveyor.
Samuel Pepys, Esq., Clerk of the Acts.
John, Lord Berkeley (of Stratton),)
Sir William Penn,) Commissioners.
Peter Pett, Esq.)

The duty of these officers, mainly, was to build ships for the Navy, to manage the shipyards, to feed and clothe and pay the crews, and to estimate the Navy's future needs and activity.

They met first on July 2, at Sir Edward Montague's, at seven in the evening, "to draw up such an order of the Council as would put us into action before our patents were passed . . . among the rest myself was reckoned one. . . At which my heart was glad." The government of Charles was being organized. The Restoration had come hardly a month before.

All the other officers were older than Pepys. Carteret was 61; Slingsby, 49; Batten over 63—probably the oldest of the seven; Berkeley, 54; Penn, 39; Pett, 50; and Pepys, 27. He was at least thirty-five years younger than the oldest of them, and twelve years younger than the next youngest, Sir William Penn. All but one had titles, and Pett was the head of a family which for a hundred years had built the ships of the Navy. All were wealthy, some very wealthy. All had country estates or London houses. Sir George Carteret, who was high in the King's favor, lodged at Whitehall in 1662, lived for a while at Deptford, down the Thames from London, and later leased "ground and house, which is extraordinary great," in Broad Street. Sir Robert Slingsby lived in Lime Street, "a fine house," hardly a third of a mile from Seething Lane. Sir William Batten, who "had a good estate [wealth] beside his office," lived at Walthamstow, in Essex. After a visit to him Pepys wrote that "he lived like a prince." Lord Berkeley had always "the best lodging." He built later in Piccadilly, which was, Evelyn writes, "a palace . . . it stood him in near £30,000; the gardens are incomparable." Penn had an estate in Ireland. Peter Pett, who for thirteen years had been director of the shipyards at Chatham southeast of London had there a house and garden, both of which Pepys thought "rich and neat . . . most handsome." Only two beside Pepys were in the Navy building, Batten and Penn, both next door to him.

Those six other officers of the Admiralty held, or gained later, places or title of distinction. One or more of them was—or became —Baron, Baronet, Knight, Member of Parliament, Privy Councellor, Justice of the Peace; Admiral, General, Colonel, Governor of Jersey, victor over the Spanish in Jamaica and over the Dutch Fleet, Commissioner of Trade and Plantations, Commissioner of Tangier, Commissioner for Fisheries, Lord Lieutenant of Ireland, Commissioner of the Duke's household, Special Ambassador to France, President of Connaught, Member of the Royal Society, Master of Trinity House, Head of the Royal Shipyards. Two wrote verses accepted in their times, and one wrote a sound treatise on Naval affairs, of which Pepys kept a copy in his library. Some had been imprisoned, exiled, and bankrupt for their loyalty to Charles. One, earlier, in the time of Charles I, had been Surveyor of the Navy, and one Comptroller, and all were experienced in naval matters. They differed in position and culture and upbringing, in ideas, in personal and business ethics, in age, in originality and strength of mind, in sympathy and understanding of those they worked with, and in the interest they took in the new young Clerk of the Acts. They were well-established, differing men. Pepys had his colleagues to learn as well as his clerkship.

* * * * * *

Sir George Carteret, Treasurer to the Navy, was a great man, powerful with the King. He was Vice-Chamberlin, M. P., a Commissioner of Trade and the Plantations. He had defended Jersey for Charles I, when he was its Governor, had lost his fortune for him, and had gone with him into exile. His family had been in Jersey for three hundred years. No one stood higher with Charles II. Hyde, the Lord Chancellor, was his intimate friend and colleague; and John Evelyn, one of the Commissioners of the Colonies, judged him to be a most able, honest man. His son, six years later, married Lady Jemima, Lord Sandwich's daughter, a marriage Pepys negotiated. Pepys tutored the very bashful, almost speechless young suitor, and his telling of the courtship is a charming seventeenth century comedy. Sir George was a man of authority and kindness and integrity. He did not like Sir William Batten's crude and arrogant practices and said so roundly in open Admiralty meetings, but he was a just man, ready, he told Pepys, "to embrace any good notions of Sir William Batten's to the King's advantage." Sir George liked Pepys, as far as he knew him, and Pepys honoured Sir George. He wrote, November 25, 1663, that Sir George "uses me mighty well to my great joy, and in our discourse took occasion to tell me . . . that I should find him in all things as kind and ready to serve me as my own brother." Yet Sir George did not have opportunity, nor was he the age, to be in any way intimate with Pepys. Pepys visited the Carteret's in 1665. When he took coach to leave "Sir George [who was 66] kissed me heartily, and my Lady, several times, with great kindness, and then the young ladies. . . ."

* * * * * *

Sir Robert Slingsby, Pepys liked best of the chief officers. He was intelligent and thoughtful and well-born; a seaman by training and inheritance (Sir Guilford, his father, lost at sea, had been Comptroller of the Navy for Charles I); a captain at twenty-two, a writer on Navy affairs; a poet in his minor way; a kind and humane man; and "good company," Pepys thought, at the office and outside. He had fought for Charles I, had been imprisoned and lost his fortune for Charles, and was with Charles II in exile. When he was appointed Comptroller he was forty-nine. It seems he took a liking to Pepys, twenty-two years his junior.

Pepys met him first September 5, 1660, and saw him the last time October 24, the next year. In the thirteen months Pepys wrote of him fifty times. The first entry tells only that at Sir William Batten's he saw "Col. Slingsby, who had now his appointment." The last entry tells that Sir Robert had died, a man Pepys loved "above all the officers and commissioners in the Navy."

To read the fifty entries Pepys made about Sir Robert, even the routine ones that tell they worked at the office together or took coach together or drank at a tavern, is to see Pepys's pleasure in being with Sir Robert and his respect for him. The more specific entries emphasize that impression.

24

They were together very often at work, at taverns, at their own houses, and at the houses of others. Plays, music, and books come in hardly at all. Many of the fifty entries tell of a morning or an afternoon or an evening at the Navy Office. Fewer tell of going on Navy business to Whitehall, or down the river to the dockyards at Deptford or Woolwich, or farther on to Portsmouth. Others tell of relaxations.

They talked about a great many things, without antagonism or gossip. They talked of the Navy. Sir Robert was interested in the history of the English Navy and the present state of it and its future, and he told Pepys his scheme for honoring sea officers by the creation of an Order of Knights of the Sea. He talked with Pepys of the Clerkship—how it might be carried on, its great usefulness, and the honorable standing the office had in times before the Commonwealth. They talked, too, of England's need of peace with Spain and war with France and Holland; of the Duke's marrying Lady Anne Hyde; of theology; of the Court and politics and the English colonies. Once at the Mitre, Sir Robert "fell into a discourse of poetry, and he did repeat some verses of his own making which were very good." Sir Robert seems to have talked with no taint of superiority or advice. To Sir Robert, Pepys was open, responsive, easy, at his best, with no awkwardness. In the Diary he never wrote even a glancing thrust against Sir Robert.

Sir Robert took Pepys to dinner at Lime Street, played bowls with him there, gave him a place to sleep when Pepys's house was upside down, had him meet his mother, Lady Slingsby, and his wife and his daughter and his brother, and he dined with Pepys and his wife. One evening he descended upon them and carried them off to see the King's new yacht, a sight they much enjoyed.

They drank their morning drafts together, and other times of the day they went to the Three Tuns, the Mitre, the Dolphin, Heaven, or "a tavern hard by." Sir Robert had wide enjoyments, not wholly those of Pepys but never those Pepys found tasteless or gross. At the Dolphin one November night in 1660, "we [Sir Robert, Pepys, and Sir William Batten] drank a great quantity of sack and did tell many merry stories, and in good humours we were all."

At Mr. Turner's house in the Navy Building, Sir Robert and Pepys and Sir William Batten and Mr. Davis "and their ladies . . . had a most neat little but costly and genteel supper" and afterward "much impertinent mirth and some singing of catches." At a great dinner given by the Lieutenant of the Tower, Sir Robert, like the others, became happily exhilarated. It was "High company; among others the Duchess of Albermarle." They drank all the afternoon, and then "toward night the Duchess and ladies went away." The men "set to it again till it was very late," so late that Pepys was "almost overcome," and was content to ride home in a coach and get to bed. Sir Robert had gone with Pepys "by coach to the Tower, to Sir John Robinson's, to dinner." Pepys was much pleased "to ride in such state into the Tower."

Later that year, in September, Pepys found Sir Robert at the Dolphin with a dozen other Navy officers and their wives and daughters. They heard "an excellent company of fiddlers" and were "exceeding merry till late," and some of them drank so heartily they were "almost gone." In many different ways, Sir Robert seems to have been "good company."

For October 22, 1661, Tuesday, Pepys wrote: "visit Sir R. Slingsby, who is fallen sick of this new disease, an ague and a fever." He went to see him the next day, and again the next. Saturday he wrote, "our Comptroller (who hath this day been sick a week), is dead; which put me into so great a trouble of mind, that all the night I could not sleep, he being a man that loved me, and had many qualities that made me to love him" (October 26, 1661).

Pepys made no further comment about Sir Robert.

* * * * * *

Lord Berkeley was an extra Commissioner of the Navy for four years, and then, after 1664, he held higher offices. He was one of the great nobles at the Court, a friend of the King, for whom he had fought and with whom he had been on the continent.

Pepys does not write of Lord Berkeley's working at the Navy Office. He writes of having "to look out the best lodgings for my Lord Berkeley," of Lord Berkeley's influence at Court and his relation with the King and the Duke, of constantly meeting him when he went on business to Whitehall, of Lord Berkeley's being " the most hot firey man . . . without any cause, that ever I saw, even to breach of civility," of his building his great mansion next the Lord Chancellor's, of his display rather than his kindness, of his good luck rather than his good sense. Even the edge of Lord Berkeley's time seldom touched Seething Lane.

Pepys only once dined with him and Lady Berkeley. At the dinner were Sir George Carteret, Sir William Batten, "two gentlemen more," and "one of the ladies of honor to the Duchesse. (No handsome woman, but a most excellent hand). A fine French dinner. . . ." When the Diary ended Lord Berkeley was a member of

26

the Privy Council and one of the three commissioners for the Duke of York's household. The Duke's secretary told Pepys the Lord Berkeley had swindled the Duke. After the Diary ends he was appointed Lord Lieutenant of Ireland, and later Ambassador to France. He started on his embassy with four coaches, three wagons, and forty horses.

Lord Berkeley as Pepys shows him seems a man loyal to the Stuarts, aristocratic, wealthy, intemperate in his talk and his certainties, fortunate in his friends, and a rather magnificent figure to represent England in some great and formal ceremony or office.

* * * * * *

Pepys's first judgment of Commissioner Pett was that he built a good ship "but...I...am unwilling to mix my future with him that is going down the wind" (September 6, 1660). Pett seemed to him discontented and greedy. He heard that Pett sold timber to the Navy under another name than his own, put his kin in high positions, and rigged his expense account to his own profit. Pepys was certain "what a knave Commissioner Pett hath been all along" (April 13, 1664). Pett was venial and weak. When Pepys did not buy shipmasts from him he accused Pepys of favoritism; Pepys flattened the accusation by a cool, factual, 1-2-3 letter. A year later Pepys and Sir William Minnes had "an angry bout" with Pett over his "absenting himself, unknown to us, from his place at Chatham." "A most false man, every day," Pepys found him, "and very full of guile." In 1667, when the Dutch broke through the Thames's defenses, captured much shipping, and took the "Royal Charles" and other ships of the Navy, Pett, who had charge of the defense, was dismissed from office and sent to the Tower. Pepys wrote that when Pett was called in before a committee of the King's Council he came "in his old clothes, and looking most sillily" (June 19, 1667). Pepys does not come well out of this, and he knew it. He says—and is sorry—that he showed Pett "no respect, but rather against him, for which God forgive me! for I mean no hurt to him ... but it [seemed] necessary I should be so in behalf of the office." Pett in much of this business was a scapegoat. Yet at the end, two years later, when Pepys and Colonel Thomas Middleton, Surveyor of the Navy, audited Pett's accounts they did "find him a very knave" (March 26, 1669). From first to last, he was to Pepys "the poor weak man" (October 23, 1667).

* * * * * *

Sir William Penn and Sir William Batten, whom by his residence he was with day after day, Pepys liked least. Sir William Batten seemed to him the coarsest element of them all in character, action, taste, speech, and thought. "Corrupt," the Duke of York's treasurer said of him.

Pepys was sure he could justify his place among the chief officers, and he was determined to. He knew that he was with men of wealth and maturity and distinction, and that he himself was not from an established family, and that he was poor and inexperienced and ignorant in what the others had already experienced. Yet he knew he was by birth a gentleman and was a Cambridge graduate, and had ability and could work and could adapt himself. Most of all, he had the bright, absolute certainty that he would succeed. He was not awed by title or position or seniority. He accepted the value of those, and gave them respect, but he was convinced of himself—brash, perhaps. He saw he had much to learn all at once about matters of which he knew quite nothing. He was not made helpless by his ignorance, not numbed; he had a path to cut and an end he would reach, and he rather thought he was the best of the seven officers. So he set to work learning what he had to learn, simple or complicated—even learning with a teacher, at five on a July morning, that 6 times 7 is 42. He was fortunate in capacity for interest about most things around him; tallow and poetry and blood transfusions and music and Norway pine and tar and books and rope making and the English tides and clothes and machines and stars. This interest in a diversity of things was alive and inherent, not assumed, and so was his interest, which was not always sympathy, in people. He had wit to see that different motives moved, hidden, in the minds of the six men he had to work with. Fortunately, again, he had the gift of being liked. He had a warmth and delight that warmed others, and he controlled or concealed his dislikes. He did not find living dreary or rigid or cold. Pepys enjoyed his life, and somehow he kept the time people spent with him from being to them a burden or tedious. He, as some people do, set things vibrating. He gave things color. He used his gifts. He had his eyes on success and worked indefatigably; and he had strength, some knowledge, good sense, and good judgment (slanted, of course, by his personality); and he submerged his asperities to private expression. So he became in time the spokesman of the Navy Office—to the Duke, to the King, to the Council, to Parliament, to the fumbling others in the office. He became by the end of the Diary the principal officer of the Navy.

52047

"... *much business appertaining*"

The first month, after he became Clerk of the Acts, Pepys's mind and time were crowded. There was his Admiralty work. He still was happily amazed at having been appointed, but work in and outside the office wore on him. "For this month or two, it is not imaginable how busy my head has been." He had cause for feeling pushed. He worked all day at the Admiralty, and the work was new and important to him and difficult. He knew nothing about ships, or details of administration, or what was the best Naval policy for England; and his knowledge of arithmetic and accounts was less than thin. But he was determined to succeed. That was primary with him in the summer of 1660.

Yet Lord Sandwich stood ahead of even his own success. To do anything he could for Lord Sandwich was his first business. It was absolute, unquestioned. It had become a habit with him and a duty and a pleasure. In July and August, 1660, Pepys did many things for Lord Sandwich. In personal matters, he helped him, for Lord and Lady Sandwich entirely trusted him; and in business matters, for Lord Sandwich was no businessman. "Before his going he [Lord Sandwich] did give me some jewells to keep for him, viz., that the King of Sweden did give him, with the King's own picture in it, most excellently done; and a brave George, [Garter] all of diamonds, and this with the greatest expressions of love and confidence that I could imagine or hope for, which is a very great joy to me" (March 4, 1661). And at his busiest time—in August, 1660—he had to arrange the swearing in of Lord Sandwich as a Clerk of the Privy Seal and of himself as deputy. He did, of course, arrange it all, most capably. Before two Secretaries of State, "my Lord and I upon our knees together took our oaths of Allegancy and Supremacy, and the Oath of the Privy Seal." He had his reward. Though his deputyship took time, "blessed be God ... I get every day I believe about £3 at the Privy Seal." Two days once brought him 40 pounds "at which my heart rejoiced for God's blessing to me." Besides all the rest, he looked after Lord Sandwich's affairs when Lord Sandwich was out of London and while he went to Holland for the King.

Pepys's kin brought him their troubles and took up his time. In the seventeenth and eighteenth centuries claims of kinship were strong, as Jane Austen's novels for one will prove, and Pepys especially felt the bond. He would not, he told his brother, "ever be lead . . . to forget or desert them in the main" (September 1, 1663). Yet, years after, he disinherited his nephew who was to have been his heir. When he was first Clerk of the Acts his mother was growing old and was given to constant complaining; she had "become a very simple woman" (August 13, 1661). His father, sixty-one years old, a quiet, withdrawing man, subdued by life, had come to leave decisions to him and to trust to him for help by judgment or money.

Pepys felt responsible for his sister Paulina, and his brothers, John and Tom. Paulina was twenty, ready for marriage but without a dowry and not attractive in looks or character; eight years later she married, with a dowry of 600 pounds from Pepys. He wrote, then, that she was "growing old and ugly," and earlier he had written frankly that he could not have her in his house and that she "stole" a pair of scissors from his wife and some books from the maid. Marriage improved appearance and character. John, eight years younger than he, in 1660 was in his first half-year at Cambridge, studying for the church, but not at all doing credit to himself or Cambridge by his way of life and his scholarship. "[My] brother John neither is the scholler nor minds his studies as I thought he would have done, but loiters away his time," he wrote three years later (August 29, 1663). Once John complained of Mrs. Pepys's disregard of him; and Pepys in the evening "walked with him in the garden, and discoursed long with him and directed him . . . how to behave himself to her, and gave him other counsel" (September 1, 1663). John lived to be thirty-six and never came to much, good or bad. Tom, a year younger than Pepys, carried on their father's tailoring shop, but badly. Tom, on the whole, was poor weak stuff; he borrowed and never repaid, and was shifty and would not give Pepys "account . . . how matters go with him in the world." Pepys judged that Tom went his way "without brains or care." The judgment had proof four years later when Tom died at thirty. It was quite Tom's way—and Pepys's—that early one morning just after Pepys's appointment, in the midst of new and heavy work, Tom came and told him that their father "had forbade him to come any more into the house." Pepys was "troubled," "did soundly chide Tom," who was in the wrong; and went late that afternoon to their father's. Pepys "discoursed with" his father and, showing the respect he always showed him, advised that Tom be taken home; "which I think he will do."

Settling the lease of his house in Axe Yard, gave another trouble. Pepys found "Many people look after my house . . . to hire it, so that I am troubled by them." Among them was Cromwell's son-in-law. In September he sold the lease and used the money, about 4 pounds, "to buy goods for my house."

Pepys found, too, that altering and furnishing his house in Seething Lane crowded his time and cost him energy and money.

HOUSEHOLDER

"In the south suburbs . . . Is best to lodge."

He came to his new house July 17, Tuesday, 1660. In Axe Yard all was ready for the moving. Monday, the day set for it, "proved very rainy weather so that I could not remove my goods." The morning of the seventeenth ("as indeed all the mornings now-a-days") he had much business besides his moving. He was kept by his business till noon, but at noon he came home, watched his goods being taken by the carts, went by coach to Seething Lane and saw the goods "set in," had supper ("a Quarter of Lamb, . . . not half roasted," from a shop), took a boat to Westminster on more business, and late that night came "on foot with a link-boy to my home, where I found my wife in bed and Jane washing the house, and Will the boy sleeping, and a great deal of sport I had before I could wake him. I to bed the first night that ever I lay here with my wife." The boy was Will Hewer, then seventeen years and eight months old.

What goods the carts carried from Axe Yard to Seething Lane, Pepys did not tell. The Diary makes plain he brought clothing, books, and a few pictures, and some primary, temporary things—beds, tables, hangings, chairs, and chests; not many of these, because he did not own many (in Axe Yard he had cramped and scanty space—three fair-sized rooms and a garret), and because he intended to buy fresh furnishing.

"Never since I was a man in the world . . ."

In the first six weeks at Seething Lane, Pepys made only small alterations and bought little; he had carpenters cut a door out of his bedroom onto the leads, and he bought "our new range" for cooking. It broke down the second day. Then, September 4, the joiners came to refloor the dining room; and the alterations began. A week later the carpenters were still at work (September 12). The joiners went; the plasterers came. By the twenty-sixth the whole house was "in a most sad pickle," the men so "at work in all the rooms [that] my wife was fain to make a bed upon the ground for her and me, and so there we lay all night." That was Tuesday, September 25. Four days later, Saturday, the plasterers were gone. All day Pepys stayed home cleaning up—"to make an end of our dirty work of the plasterers, and indeed my kitchen is now so handsome I do not repent of all the trouble that I have been put to." Yet the next night he went to bed "without prayers, my house being every where foul above stairs."

Monday, the first of October, the plaster was dry enough to justify Pepys's and his father's talking over what hangings would be best for the downstairs rooms; but putting up hangings was far off, for that afternoon the painters began "to do their work." After five vigorous days, they left, having done that work to Pepys's content; and, at last, at the end of a month of utter inconvenience "because of our house being always in the painters' or other peoples' hands" (part of the time it rained), Pepys was glad to see his house likely again to be clean (October 5).

The workmen, in seventeenth century fashion, came early, even before six, and stayed "till 10 or 11 at night" (September 28). Pepys thought they needed looking after; at times their "laziness do much trouble me." So, now and then, though not often, he stayed at home. He found that some of the workmen were lazy and some were not; and after he had talked with them he liked many of them and "did give them drink and very merry with them, it being my luck to meet with a sort [group] of drolling workmen." But Pepys wanted his house free of any workmen above stairs and down.

To Pepys, the six months after May, 1660 were wearing. He had too much work and little variety of life, and he was twenty-seven. The importance to him of his appointment and the intensity and the narrow range of his actions—office and house—kept him from much he enjoyed, and rasped his control, and upset his body. He was, he wrote August 10, "unable to think of anything, because of my constant attendance [at the office of the Privy Seal] after I have done at the Navy Office ... Never since I was a man in the world was I ever so great a stranger to public affairs as now I am, having not read a new book or anything like it, or enquiring after any news, or what the Parliament do, or in any wise how things go." Except for business, he saw none of his friends. He had "neglected to write letters [even] in answer to many." For three months he had not had time to see a play, nor time and mood as he had a year later to go, in April, "at night into the garden to play on my flageolette, it being moonshine." Until August 20, he did not bring home his lute from Lord Sandwich's, where he had left it in May. Often he was in pain; often—and he was sorry for it— he was short-tempered with his wife. He was thoroughly upset. One evening in November, after he and his wife had gone to bed "in a quarrel," he was troubled with a dream that his wife was dead, "which made me that I slept ill all night."

"Put money in thy purse."

Joiners, plasterers, painters did finish. The strangeness and the pressure at the Admiralty and the Privy Seal lessened. He and his wife began furnishing the house.

Even while he had been waiting for his appointment, before he had left Axe Yard, Pepys had started buying. He had bought in July "two fine prints of Ragotti from Rubens" at the new Exchange in the Strand, and the new kitchen range: two ends of his domestic rainbow. After he was in the house he bought more books, some from the booksellers in Westminster Hall; and after his appointment he began getting wall-hangings and fabrics for upholstering chairs and for bed curtains, and he and his wife went to a stationer to choose "pictures for our house," and he had Lily's portrait of Lord Sandwich copied for his study at a cost of 3 pounds 10 shillings.

At first his wife did mainly routine buying, but he found she had good sense and good taste in buying of all sorts. With the "bed and furniture [she got for] her chamber [he was] very well pleased" (October 2); and the next day he had her go "abroad ... to buy more furniture for her house"; and a week later she still was buying "household stuff." He himself, with high reach, was seeing "about gilded leather for my dining room." He carried out that high plan; on October 19 the dining room had "green serge hanging and gilt leather, which is very handsome." He and his wife kept on buying innumerable things large and small: fire irons, pewter sconces for the hall, red hangings for the elegance of a new, red bedroom, more curtains, and good dishes and tables and chairs. He had some of his books gilded, and, in time, he added new mantles, a window for the cellar, railings about the leads, and much else.

He had gifts for his house: a good amount of old pewter, 5 pounds worth, from his father; "a brave Turkey carpet" from a captain in the royal Navy; "a cupp of lignum vitae" (hard, black-green wood) made by his cousin, Thomas Pepys the turner, "for a token"; a set of silver plates, a silver flagon, and other things, most of which pleased his taste and were useful.

Furnishing a house cost more than he had thought it would. Pepys had his income as Clerk and his fees from the Privy Seal office and money—about 41 pounds—from his house in Axe Yard. Still, cost went beyond planning. "My layings out upon my house in furniture are so great that I fear I shall not be able to go through them without breaking one of my bags of £100. I having but £200 yet in the world." That he wrote the first of October. At the end of October, his "mind [was] very heavy ... for the great-ness of my late expenses, insomuch that I do not think I have about £150 clear money in the world, but I have, I believe, got a great deal of good household stuff." He was emerging. December 31, he summed up the year: "I take myself now to be worth £300 clear money, and all my goods and all manner of debts paid, which are none at all ... I do live in one of the houses belonging to the Navy Office, as one of the principal officers ... in a most handsome and thriving condition. Blessed be Almighty God for it." So his first half year in Seething Lane has the happy ending.

"... it do please me very well"

Until the end of the Diary, Pepys kept on altering his house, but he never again wrote as he had in the first six months of change. The alteration became, even in a year, part of his leisure, a dream increasingly realized, proof of his success and of his con-quest over mediocrity. The changes added convenience to his ways of living, and grace and beauty to his life. They met a con-stant wish of his for perfection. Besides, he learned to lessen the upheavals by storing his goods, shifting his wife and the maids to the country, and lodging next door with Sir William Penn. He came, it seems, to enjoy having the work done. In 1661 (March 25) he wrote, it "do please me very well" that carpenters had begun "a new pair of stairs up out of my parlor," which was likely to keep him two months "all in dirt." He repeated that it pleased him "well ... that my workmen have begun to-day," though he "could not get up but by a ladder." He felt an almost pleasant discomfort.

He had much that mood while he made large changes in 1662. Saturday, July 12, he and his wife got up "by five o'clock, and put things in my house in order to be laid up, against my workmen come on Monday to take down the top of my house." The officers had been permitted to have a storey added. Monday, though the workmen were untiling the roof "in order to its rising higher," he went on studying his arithmetic in the morning, and in the evening took a few turns in the garden with his wife. Tuesday the house was "all open at top." "About bedtime it fell a-raining." Pepys saw no help for it.

The rain kept on for almost a month. The end of the first week he and his wife took the room Sir William Penn offered, "my own house being so foul that I cannot lie there any longer." (Yet just then it came into his head to have his dining-room wainscoated, "which will be very pretty.") The rain kept on. Sunday morning, when the rain was so furious the inside of his house was as wet as the open street, Pepys, worried, went over to his house. He found in it not one dry foot, upstairs or down, and he "fitted himself for dirt," and in the solid rain moved his books to his office. Then he and wife had a dinner of calf's head and bacon, and she agreed, though not eagerly, to go to Brampton, to his father's. She did go the twenty-eighth and stayed two months. When she came back, he "found her and her maid and a dogg well, and herself grown a little fatter than she was.") All the afternoon he dabbed again in the water, and in the evening at his office he wrote up his journal and read over his oaths against the drinking of wine and going to plays, "as I am obliged every Lord's day"; then being very dirty and "in fear of having catched cold," he went to their room, washed, and slept. The next day he found he had caught cold, but it was quite cured or was forgotten in a trip down the Thames to Greenwich, where the sun shone.

Fair weather came early in the first week of August. The men got to tiling the roof, and on Friday, the eleventh, Pepys was at ease because his house was quite tiled. He was pleased with the new storey.

He went on making changes. His wife's closet, when it was altered, would be "very pretty"; "a chimney-piece made in my upper dining-room chamber" was good; so was his dining-room wainscoat; he was afraid purple wall-hangings in his study would "be too sad for that melancholly little room," but he liked the color; and pulling down "the partition between the entry and the boy's room . . . to lay it all into one . . . will . . . make my coming in more pleasant." It all took time. So he was not "in the last dirt" until November was half over. Then November 15, 1662, he "saw my painters make an end of my house this night, which is my great joy."

36

Through all the dampening and derangement, Pepys took things as they came. The discomfort in the house and in his mind was not personal and not always present as it had been in 1660. The sun— after his forty days—did come out, as he had been sure it would when, not often, he had philosophized over his deluge.

* * * * * *

One day in July 1662, the same year, when "the weather [was] cold and likely to rain," Pepys took boat to Greenwich; and after "landing at the riverside somewhere among the reeds," he went to Captain Cocke's estate and walked with him in the garden. The apricots were ripe there. He saw Mrs. Cocke, "still pretty" but just then angry with her husband, which put Pepys so "clear out of countenance that [he] was sorry" he had come. "So after I had eat still some more fruit I took leave of her in the garden plucking apricots for preserving." Vivid (Pepys saw what he looked at), and quite idyllic; and not the mood or the prose of his disturbed summer, two years before.

By the end of the Diary, in late 1668, he had come to like tinkering about his home. One quiet Sunday in November, he "lay long, with mighty content; and so rose," and after his wife had gone out, he spent time "Knocking up nails and making little settlements in my house, till noon, and then eat a bit of meat in the kitchen." That afternoon and evening he was at his office for awhile, had his wife read to him, talked with Will Hewer, supped, and "so after supper, to bed," (November 22, 1668).

Dragons

Pepys, living as he did separated from others only by partitions and ceiling, had household alarms and defeats; only one defeat, really. Mrs. Davis and her husband, who was in the Admiralty Office, came about the first of October, 1660, to "lodgings" next Pepys. In some way Pepys's use of the leads disturbed the lady. When Pepys came home the evening of October 29, he found she had locked up his door out onto the leads, which put him "into so great a disquiet that [he] could not sleep till morning at it." The next day he took his complaint to the Navy officers, but they all agreed they were "unwilling to meddle in anything that may anger my Lady Davis."

The Davises were a recurring trial. One morning in November he saw "a great deal of foul water come into my parlor from under the partition between me and Mr. Davis." Pepys went to Mr. Davis and told "him of it and he did seem very ready to have it stopt," and did stop it. Then, too, Mr. Davis carried to his own house carpenters who had come to work for Pepys. Pepys went and brought them back; Mr. Davis questioned; Pepys was firm "that they were come on purpose to do some work with me." It ended with Mr. Davis's being "well pleased" at the explanation. Fortunately, the Davis's left Seething Lane early that spring (March 18, 1661).

In the same October, 1661, the twentieth, Pepys found sure proof when he went down into his own cellar that the vault in Mr. Turner's cellar, the cesspool, was full and was overflowing into his. Pepys wrote, "I shall have it helped." He did. Five days later the vaults had been cleaned.

For years, at intervals, Sir John Minnes, who followed Sir Robert Slingsby as Comptroller, brought out his complaints. The storey Pepys had added, he said, "blinded all his lights" [darkened his windows]; and one of Pepys's alterations "stopped up his garden door"; Pepys's "best lodging chamber" belonged to him and he wanted it back; and when Pepys's workmen put up a railing on Pepys's leads, Sir John "did spy them and fell a-swearing, which [Pepys] took no notice of, but was vexed . . . to the very heart." Sir John was an old Cavalier of the time of Charles I, an Admiral. He was learned in science—seemed to "know something . . . of chymistry," wrote Pepys, and of the sea, and had other gifts. He then was sixty-two or more, and a little broken in vigor. Pepys won over him each time. Each time, Sir John swore on, complained, grumbled, and gave in—almost good naturedly. Pepys did get exasperated. He called Sir John, in the Diary, an "old cockscomb," "a doating fool," "a jester or a ballad maker," and always thought him "quite incapable at business." Others were more harsh with Sir John. Yet at bottom Pepys liked him. He was "most excellent pleasant company . . . and brought many fine expressions of Chaucer, which he doats on mightily"; and he had some judgment in pictures, and wrote fair *vers de societe.*

One happy January day in 1666, in a "company" at Lord Brouncker's, the Extra Commission of the Navy, after Pepys and his "dear Mrs. Knipp" had sung together and she, alone, had sung "her little Scotch song of Barbary Allen . . . and in perfect pleasure I was to hear her sing," Sir John, sixty-eight, "in the highest pitch of mirthe," made their "mirthe" the completer" by the best "mimicall tricks that ever I saw, and the most excellent pleasant company he is, and the best minique." So Pepys, having won indeed all the battles, came in the end to write that Sir John was "a very good, harmless, honest, gentleman, though not fit for business."

Most of his neighbors in the Navy Office, Pepys found to be good neighbors. He had, though, a householder's usual encounters with a few proximate, neighborhood dragons.

"Full many a glorous morning ..."

Pepys had energy, fresh taste, a plan, and a fair amount of money. He could learn, and he liked to learn, and he was sure he ought to learn. He was hardheaded, tenacious; he carried on what he started. As the Diary shows, he had excited satisfaction when he got the results he was after.

He was an artist. He had imagination. He believed in the reality and the need of perfection. Sometimes he caught sight, as a poet does, of its shining edge; and he knew that though perfection always escaped him he could always keep the pursuit. The bettering of his house was to him, in its way, a kind of poetry.

ST. OLAVE'S HART STREET

Founded XI century was rebuilt
Late XII century the crypt of this period
Also parts of the west wall remain.
Richard and Robert C. 1450 A.D. built
The church which survived the Great Fire
1666 A.D. and was grievously damaged by
Enemy action 1941 A.D.

St. Olave's Hart Street—church, churchyard, tower, vestry, and other spaces and buildings—is at the southwest corner of Seething Lane and Hart Street, across from where Pepys lived when he was Clerk of the Acts, and a little north of it. The large Naval housing, in which was Pepys's office and home after 1660, was directly across from it.

Today, Seething Lane is a narrow, stone-bound way between warehouses and offices, though its name (given before 1200) has country meaning. *Lane* is the Old London name for a path or road usually so narrow one cart could not pass another in it nor a cask of wine "be rolled along it transversely with one man at each end." A London lane might shrink to 4 feet or 5 or 7, or widen to 12 or 14 or even 18. It joined two streets. The Lane was *Seething* Lane because along it grain once had been threshed, grain which came from fields beyond the high City walls, close at the east. *Seething* is from an Old English word meaning *chaff, siftings, bran.*

In Elizabeth's time, "divers fair and large houses," wrote Stow, were built there, for Sidon lane, as he calls it, was close to the Royal Palace of the Tower: "one by Sir John Allen, sometime mayor of London, . . . Sir Francis Walsingham, knight, principal secretary to the queen's majesty . . . that now is." There, too, were Lord Howard of Effingham, and the Earl of Essex. From Seething Lane, Essex set out on his fatal campaign in Ireland.

Stow names some of the monuments in the "proper parish church of St. Olave," at least four of which remain. St. Olave's was the official church of the Clothworkers and the Ironmongers companies, and the Masters and Brothers of Trinity House attended its services each Trinity Sunday.

In Pepys's time Seething Lane was a narrow street in the city; possibly it should be called a partly built-up suburban street. The Tower was about a quarter of a mile east and the active City far off to the west. Hart Street was a *street* because it was wider than a lane; and it was *Hart* probably because hearthstones once were sold there.

St. Olave's Hart Street is an old, historic, active foundation. The present church is gray stone, darkened by smoke and London air. Today the church buildings are beautiful. For 900 years St. Olave's has done great service; "probably" might best be put with the 900, for the date of the beginning is not known. The parish existed before 1109; that year Queen Mathilda, the Saxon wife of Henry I, held land in the parish of "St. Olave's by the Tower." A church dedicated to St. Olaf of Norway as early as this one usually was a thank-offering for deliverance from Danish raiders. St. Olaf was Norway's patron saint, a defender against enemies. He has had his cathedral, built above his tomb at Trondhjem, for close to a thousand years. In 1951, when restoration began after the bombings of 1940, King Haakon VII of Norway laid the King's Stone, the Restoration Stone; and the Bishop of Trondhjem brought from the Saint's tomb a carved and inscribed fragment of stone which has been built into the church "alongside the King's Stone." On the tower is a second staff for flying the Norwegian flag with the flag of England. The church was rehallowed in April, 1954, after the main restoring was complete.

Part of the church—the crypt and some of the walls—was built in the eleventh century; part of the west wall in the fifteenth century; parts—the vestry is one—in the sixteenth and early seventeenth centuries; and much between 1950 and today.

In September 1940, the explosion of a bomb near the church shattered its windows. April 17, 1941, a direct hit smashed the interior into rubble and weakened the north and east walls, and so made the church unusable. May 11, the same year, an incendiary bomb burned out the church tower and the baptistry and other buildings. It calcined furnishings and monuments not safely stored, and even melted the peal of eight bells back into bell metal.

In 1951, the restoring began. The belfry and the vestry and the crypt and the enclosing wall were rebuilt much as they had been, or were strengthened or cleaned or in some way brought closer to their best condition; the interior of the church was in part rebuilt as it had been and in part redesigned and enriched. Old monuments and furnishings, stored for safety, were again put in place, and much that was new was added. The wood used inside the church—the organ screen, the reredos, the roof, the main seatings, and other furnishings—are for the most part light oak; some of the stone and wood is carved and gilded and colored in Norse designs. The empty window spaces were filled by stained glass less dark in colors than the old windows had been and so letting in the greater light needed now, when all about the church are tall, darkening buildings. A Memorial Porch was built at the south entrance. The bells were recast from the melted bell metal, recast in the same foundry—the Whitechapel Bell Foundry—which had made the original peal in 1662 and 1694. Today, sixteen years after the bombing, St. Olave's is again a rich and beautiful church.

In the centuries before 1941, St. Olave's—*St. Olave juxta turrim Londini*—had a notable history. It begins as a tradition that before the Norman Conquest a small wooden church stood where St. Olave's stands today. Light touches the church's history more surely in the fifteenth century, though fourteenth century stonework and a door of about that time are parts of the present building. By the sixteenth century, St. Olave's had become an "ancient and stately Parish Church, a spacious and beautiful church." In 1585, Sir Philip Sidney's daughter was baptised there. Elizabeth held thanksgiving in St. Olave's on her release from the Tower of London four hundred years ago, and she gave bellropes of silk to All Hallows Staining, joined now with St. Olave's, because its bells had rung so valiantly the day she was released. She stands in the new East Window with two bells of the Church at her feet. Her dress is blue-green, embroidered with an all-over vinelike design in gold. She wears a sort of gold stomacher, a high close white ruff, and a very noble deep blue underskirt. She holds in her right hand a small roundish red fan. "The fans used by Elizabeth," Miss Strickland has written, "were made of feathers, set in a rich handle, and in form resembling a modern [1844] hand-screen. The following is the description of one of those graceful accessories to the royal toilet, which was presented to her majesty by Sir Francis Drake, as a New Year's gift:—A fan of feathers, white and red, enamelled with a half-moon of mother of pearls, within that a half-moon garnished with sparks of diamonds, and a few seed pearls on the one

42

side; having her majesty's picture within it." (vol. 6, p.460, *Lives of the Queens*, Agnes Strickland).

For two hundred and ninety years, the Princess Elizabeth's release from the Tower was commemorated by a service at St. Olave's and a dinner under the authority of a chosen "General." In 1768 the General was Abraham Newman, one of the Wardens of the Church, and, as well, "a partner in the firm of Tea Merchants whose tea was unceremoniously cast overboard in Boston Harbour." The firm, founded in 1650, "one of the oldest in The City, still flourishes" at 14 Creechurch Lane. His memorial on the wall of the Church was destroyed by the bombing. Many notable persons were members of its congregation: men and women distinguished by birth, or by position in the Church, the Army, the Navy, or in science, commerce, law, or public affairs. In 1665, 326 who had died of the Plague were buried in the Church or in the churchyard. From the Great Fire of 1666, which burned 87 of the 109 churches in the City, St. Olave's though its burning seemed certain, miraculously—to Pepys—came out safe.

November 10, 1669, Elizabeth Pepys died of fever just after the Diary ends, close to her twenty-ninth birthday. She is buried below the monument which Pepys designed. High in the north wall of the chancel, lighted by east windows, her white marble bust, stained today by 300 years, leans forward and with head turned a little looks as Pepys planned toward the Naval Gallery, where he sat on Sundays. Her expression is eager, joyous, changing, intelligent; her hair, in light curls; her features, delicate and sensitive. The bust, by John Bushnell, is a charming portrait; it somehow seems poised in a moment of life rather than held solidly in stone. Even Baedeker calls it "charming." During the Blitz the monument was safe in the crypt of St. Paul's.

Anyone writing of St. Olave's or seeing it or thinking of it, inevitably comes back to Pepys. For forty years he was part of it, often an important part, and St. Olave's was part of his personal and official life. He writes of it well over 250 times. In the Diary, by 1662, St. Olave's was "our church" and the Rev. Dr. Mills, for thirty-two years its rector (1657-1689), was "our minister," whom Pepys and his wife heard on Sunday and whom Pepys, generally, thought a "good and able preacher." Pepys, and Elizabeth Pepys, went to St. Olave's Sunday morning unless he was of necessity out of town (and, away, he kept up his church going, or unless, as seldom happened, he was driven by much immediate business or was ill or St. Olave's, like other London churches, was closed by the Plague). On September 9, 1666, the first Sunday after the Great Fire, Pepys went twice to St. Olave's. In the morning "The church was mighty full; . . . most strangers." The minister "made a melancholy but good sermon; and many and most . . . cried." In the afternoon, "to church again, and there preached [the] Dean [of Rochester]; but methinks a bad, poor sermon, though proper for the time; not eloquent."

Pepys stayed a member of St. Olave's after he resigned as Secretary to the Admiralty in 1689, and even after he went, in ill health, to live in Clapham with William Hewer, about 1700. Thirty-four years from the death of his wife, he was buried in St. Olave's, June 4, 1703. Dr. George Hicker, Dean of Worcester, wrote to Arthur Charlett, Master of University College, Oxford, who knew Pepys in the Royal Society and outside it, "Last night, at 9 o'clock, I did the last office for your and my good friend Mr. Pepys, at St. Olave's Church, where he was laid in a vault of his own making, by his wife and brother." It was under the monument to his wife in the chancel, "near the communion table," as the register of the church states. At the first Evensong of the rededicated church, prayers were read from the *Prayer Book* Pepys used at the services in St. Olave's.

OTHER CHURCHES

What Pepys wrote of services at St. Olave's is for the most part routine—stenciled comment. His terms are general, vague, or are undescriptive negatives. He writes that St. Olave's had no organ and twice he was "minded" to give it "a pair": he never did; the psalms there were not read but sung, rather badly; toward the end of 1660, "Mr. Mills did begin to nibble at the Common Prayer, by saying *Glory be to the Father*, &c. after he had read the two psalms." Sometimes Pepys gave the text of a sermon, sometimes suggested the doctrinal drift. He usually noted the number and quality of those at any church he visited. "Very few people and few of any rank," he wrote after going to St. Gabriel's Fenchurch. Such writing runs to pattern.

He does make acute comments on some services. Robert Frampton, afterward Bishop of Gloucester, gave at St. Olave's "to my great joy . . . I think the best sermon for goodness and oratory . . . that ever I heard in my life. The truth is, he preaches the most like an apostle that ever I heard man. His text was . . ."—and he gives the text. The next Sunday Pepys sent his wife "by coach to hear Mr. Frampton preach, which I had a mighty desire she should." Pepys seldom has such enthusiasm about a sermon. Mr. Frampton did not preach that day, "which I am sorry for." Another sermon was "a cold sermon of a young man that never had preached before"; another, "a most insipid coxecomb" preached; another was by "a bawling young Scot . . . to whose . . . voice I am never to be reconciled." Once "our lecturer made a sorry silly sermon," and once at the Abbey Church in Bath "a vain, pragmatical fellow preached a ridiculous, affected sermon, that made me angry" (June 14, 1668). But there was at Bath a good organ, and some gentlemen sitting next Pepys sang well. He went again that afternoon to the Abbey "where the same idle fellow preached; and I slept through the sermon." The French Chapel of the Savoy, between

45

the Strand and the Thames, used then and now as the parish church, he thought a "pretty place." This chapel of the old palace, "again raised and beautifully built . . . about the year 1509" (Stow: *London*), today is a "dim little building lying low in a small church-yard and surrounded by the white-tiled" backs of great hotels and offices (1956). Pepys was surprised that the minister at the Savoy read the service in French and preached with his hat off. At Lady Sandwich's family chapel, near Brampton, he heard her chaplain preach a "seraphic kind of sermon, too good for an ordinary congregation." Such a comment is sharp, yet most of the entries on church-going are pointed only when unusual facts and unexpected happenings come in which have little to do with the service. His Diary likes the odd rather than the religious. It is hard to unify the slight, rather cool, rather aloof tabulations with the self-forgetful delight he had when, say, he was early in his garden at his lute, or with his, at times, impassioned feeling about music, and his interest in people.

Whenever his curiosity or his personal concern did sharpen he gave a lively account. He did about the building of the Naval gallery in St. Olave's. A month after he became Clerk, even though pushed by his work, he went to the church; picked out a "place to build . . . a gallery" for the officers and their families and servants; got a promise it should be built "speedily"; and when he saw the work was lagging set his own men to push it ahead and watched them day by day. He gives much good detail about this gallery-building. Though it was "yet not quite finished . . .[he and Sir William Batten] went to Church into our new gallery, the first time it was used. . . There came after us Sir W. Pen, Mr. Davis, and his eldest son. There being no woman this day, we sat in the foremost pew, and behind us our servants, and I hope it will not always be so, it not being handsome for our servants to sit so equal with us" (10 November, 1660). A week later, for the first time, Elizabeth Pepys and Lady Batten together "came to sit in their new pew." To Pepys all this uninspiring action was lively matter. One moment of a Sunday two days before Christmas in 1660 is aromatic: "In the morning to Church, where our pew [was] all covered with rose-mary and baize"—a fragrance of rosemary and laurel leaves that lasts.

The Diary brightens, too, when Pepys saw a handsome woman at St. Olave's or sat close to one not so handsome; and—with another tone—when one Sunday from his pew he "espied Pemberton [the dancing master] leer upon my wife all through the sermon."

In Plague time he was much disturbed—and his phrasing shows it—to hear the death-bell of St. Olave's "toll and ring so often today (July 30, 1665), either for deaths or burials; I think five or six times." And he was fearful—"was frighted"—after the Plague had passed to find that the levelled earth of St. Olave's churchyard was a foot or two higher because of the added coffins below.

Even when Pepys went to another church, he was not led by change of place into writing vividly of its service. As at St. Olave's, his interest came chiefly from the unchurchly. Instinctively his interest rose at novelty, even trivial novelty: the rope about the middle of "the fryer" preaching in Portuguese at the Queen's Chapel; My Lord's anthem being sung in the Chapel Royal, and the concert of 24 violins being played there, and King Charles's beating time to an anthem; a glowing stained-glass window; a eunuch's unEnglish voice; a fiddle out of tune; and at Whitehall on Sunday, January 3, 1661, "trumpets and kettle-drums and other drums, which are much cried up, though I think it dull, vulgar music." Such things engaged him. When all was usual, Pepys, if he wrote anything, catalogued, with no comment or a barren one. His mind set to work when he faced the new; and he was not concerned with judgment of its value.

Other times, of other churches, he wrote dully. After going to St. Margaret's Church (August 5, 1660), where he was married, he recorded only a passing fact; there, for the first time he heard the Book of Common Prayer read in a church. Of St. Lawrence Jury —"a very fine church"—he recorded only that "a gentleman sat in the pew I by chance sat in, that sang most excellent" and that it turned out he had been at Pepys's old school: another fact. After he went to a morning service at St. Clement Danes "by appointment" with Captain Cocke to hear Mr. Alsopp, whom Cocke had often praised, Pepys recorded flatly that Mr. Alsopp did not "come up to my expectation," a phrasing bare of the colors he had given the dinner of Friday that week with the Captain and his wife, a "lady . . . of great beauty." The meetings of the Royal Society were full of excitement for him. "It is a most acceptable thing to hear their discourse, and see their experiments; which were this day upon the nature of fire, and how it goes out in a place where the ayre is not free, and sooner out where the ayre is exhausted, which they showed us by an engine on purpose." (This was written February 15, 1665, the day he was "unanimously elected and admitted" as a member of the Society.) Of St. Bride's, the parish church of his father and mother, across the lane from their home and the shop, the church where he had been christened, in the churchyard of which he played when he was a child, and where his mother had her pew and eight of his brothers and sisters were buried before the Fire, he wrote ten times and said nothing. When he buried his brother Tom in the church, he wrote a live comment though not at all related to St. Bride's: "Lord! to see how the world makes nothing of the memory of a man, an houre after he is dead! And, indeed, I must blame myself; for though at the sight of him dead and dying, I had real grief for a while, while he was in my sight, yet presently after, and ever since, I have had very little grief indeed for him" (18 March, 1664).

Pepys did not care for St. Dunstan's in the East. Once and incidentally, however, the church pleasantly centers attention. Pepys tells without color that a Sunday afternoon in August, 1663, (the ninth) after dinner he led Lady Batten "through the streets by the hand to St. Dunstan's Church, hard by us . . . and heard an excellent sermon . . . upon *Remember Lot's wife.*" St. Dunstan's in the East—there was a St. Dunstan's in the West—was less than a quarter of a mile from Lady Batten's home. And so he would have led her by the hand south down Seething Lane, west on Tower Street a short way, and then by Church Lane to the church. It would have been a promenade to see.

—2—

Though on Sunday morning Pepys went steadily to the service at St. Olave's, in the afternoon sometimes he "ranged about to many churches" and "heard a little" or much at each. Even on weekdays he might "look in" at a church and stay three minutes or an hour—from the Temple to the Tower and from the open Moorfields at the north of the City to Southwark across the river. A frosty Sunday in December, 1661, Pepys dined with Lady Sandwich at her house just east of the Temple, a mile down the river from Seething Lane. . . Then "after a good deal of good discourse with my Lady . . . I went away up and down into all the churches almost between that place and my home," not an unusual pilgrimage for him. Another Sunday in spring two years later, "This morning till churches were done, I spent going from one church to another and hearing a bit here and a bit there. So . . . to dinner" (March 16, 1662).

About such visitings to other churches he wrote little, but of one Sunday in October he gave a full and unusual account. October 2, 1664, "my wife not being well to go to church I walked . . . through the City, putting in at several churches, among others at

48

Bishopsgate." He had intended seeing the Quakers "who, they say, do meet every Lord's day of the Mouth" tavern outside Bishopsgate, but he "could see none stirring." He walked on across Moorfields, about a mile and a quarter, to the ancient church of St. James's Clerkenwell. There he sat in the "next pew to the fair Butler, who indeed is a most perfect beauty . . . and one I do much admire." In the afternoon, when he had dined with Lady Sandwich near Gray's Inn, he went back to the Clerkenwell church but the lady was not there. At home again, his wife, shrewdly, was "angry with me for . . . gadding about to look after beauties, she told me plainly." Pepys and she as usual "made all peace" in the end. Two years later he walked to St. Lawrence Church "to have one look at Betty Mitchell . . ., a young wench . . . and very pretty."

Pepys went to more than thirty churches in London and to others outside it, most of them Anglican. Their names ranged through the alphabet from All Hallows Barking to Saint Sepulchre. Besides, he went to the Temple Church, to St. Peters *ad Vinculm* in the Tower, to the School Church of St. Paul's, often to the Chapel Royal—the King's—and to the Queen's Catholic Chapel in St. James's Place, and to Westminster Abbey and St. Paul's Cathedral.

At the French Church in the Savoy, Pepys had been vastly surprised that the minister preached with his hat off. This hat wearing is one of the minor confusions the seventeenth century has for the twentieth. Men wore hats, or a century earlier, caps, all day long. Hats were part of usual dress. A man put his on fairly soon after he got out of bed, and he kept it on as he did his shoes or his coat while he ate or worked or read or paid a visit or went to church or to the theatre. Often it was worn for warmth and against drafts. Pepys was sure in September, 1664, that though he was wearing his periwig he "got a strange cold in my head, by flinging off my hat at dinner and sitting with the wind in my neck." Taking off one's hat was sign of reverence or respect. A man doffed his before a person of notably higher rank than he. A well-brought-up boy would not wear his before age or dignity. Lord Chancellor Clarendon wrote (*On the decay of respect paid to Age*) that in his younger days he never kept his hat on before those older than himself except at dinner. A minister wore his in the pulpit, though he might or might not raise it when he named the Deity; and a friend might perhaps take his off, for a little, in friendly talk.

The Earl of Sussex, grand chamberlain to Elizabeth and her ambassador with the Archduke Charles of Austria, wrote to the Queen that the Archduke had said: "By your manner of dealing with me,

49

I do think myself bound (wherewith he put off his cap), to honour, love and serve her majesty while I live." Pepys, when he was one of the Committee of Tangier, wrote that "it was mighty strange methought to find myself sit here in Committee with my hat on, while Mr. Sherwin [Clerk of the Committee] stood bare as a clerke, with his hat off to his Lord Ashly [Privy Councillor, Chancellor of the Exchequer, and later the great Earl of Shaftesbury] and the rest, but I thank God I think myself never a whit the better man for all that" (January 17, 1665). A barrister created Sargeant-at-Law after more than fifteen years of service, wore his cap, a white tight-fitting coif, even before the King. Othello could speak unbonneted to the greatest as their equal; and Iago off-capped, to show his humble honesty. Nightcaps merely continued the day's head covering. Elizabeth Pepys made "caps" for her husband.

THE ABBEY AND ST. PAUL'S

Axe Yard, where Pepys lived from the summer of 1658 to that of 1660, was a quarter of a mile north of Westminster Abbey. Pepys went to sermons and vespers at the Abbey; walked in its precincts; heard there for the first time "organs in a cathedral"; saw Charles crowned there; once, years later, sang in its choir; very often made appointments at it; in at least one waiting-time walked among the Abbey tombs "with great pleasure" (September 12, 1664); and to give tang to his thirty-sixth birthday, February 23, 1669, kissed the mouth of the 200 year-old mummy, for centuries half-exposed, of Queen Catherine of Valois, Henry the V's and Shakespeare's "dear Kate." He wrote at least thirty times of the Abbey, chiefly passing allusions to it as a convenient meeting place. It was part of his usual life.

Westminster—the town—was hurrying, varied, easy of access by walking or by boat, with noble old buildings and good taverns and all kinds of good shops. It was close to the King's Palace, to the houses of nobles, and to the crowded, more common streets. Westminster Hall, by the Abbey, Pepys names at least 350 times—the great hall of William Rufus and the Edwards and Richard II, 600 years old, and 290 feet long, 70 feet wide, and a 100 high; where the law courts sat for 500 years; where Charles I had been condemned; on the roof of which Pepys, in 1661, saw the heads of Cromwell, Bradshaw, and Ireton, fixed on spikes; in which he watched the Coronation banquet and saw the King's Champion "all in armour on horseback" ride into the Hall and fling his gauntlet down as a challenge; where at the same feast he and Mr. Creed got themselves "four rabbits and a pullet and . . . some bread," and ate them "at a stall," and then "took a great deal of pleasure to go up and down, and look upon the ladies, and to hear the musique of all sorts, but above all, the 24 violins" (April 23, 1661). Pepys writes of Westminster Hall in the first month of the Diary and in the last. He was familiar with it. His early clerkship, the summer of 1658, was at the office of the Court of the Exchequer, in New Palace Yard, just north of the Hall. January 28, 1660 he dined in Heaven, the oldest tavern of the Hall, at least as old as 1540, "on a breast of mutton all alone," and another time that year he and Mr. Creed "to *Hell* to drink our morning draught." Hell was a large tavern, "at that time kept by a Mr. Duke," underneath the Exchequer, with a door opening into the northwest corner of the Hall. Hell was the cant name for the Hall's basement. In the Hall were bookstalls and stalls where other "things [were] to be sold" (May 15, 1660). Against the west wall some houses of gentlemen had been built, from the upper "parlours" of which doors opened to galleries inside the Hall. It was from such a gallery that Lady Fairfax watched the trial of Charles I and, when the judges brought their accusation of him "in the name of the people of England," cried out to them "It is a lie—not half the people!"

After he was Clerk of the Acts, Pepys went often to Westminster. A pleasant way of going was by boat, 2½ miles up the river from Tower Stairs—past what now is Billinsgate Market, beneath London Bridge against the swift current made dangerous by close-set piers, past wharves and landing cranes and warehouses for coal and oil and ship-chandlery, past the Temple gardens "banking on the river," as Stow phrases it, past the houses of the nobility, fruit trees and flowers and grass growing to the river's edge, past the half mile of Whitehall Palace, and so to Westminster Stairs. Pepys often took boat back to London Bridge and walked, beyond, the three-quarters of a mile to his office. Pepys liked to walk.

For close to ten years, his years from six to seventeen, Pepys went to St. Paul's School, just east and south of St. Paul's Cathedral. On most days of those years he walked past the Cathedral. It became established firmly as part of his everyday experience. It was *there;* it always would be there. And seeing the great Church became so natural, so much taken for granted, that he hardly noticed it at all.

Before the Fire, he wrote of the Cathedral only 15 or 16 times, generally to give some small, unusual item about it or to tell of a City celebration in it. He "put in at Paul's" one Sunday in April because "our minister, Mr. Mills was preaching before my Lord Mayor." That is all he told of the incident (April 7, 1661). Six months later he was interested (October 29, 1661) that the new "Lord Mayor . . . brings up again the custom of Lord Mayors going the day of their installment to Paul's and walking round the Cross, and offering something at the altar." St. Paul's Cross—"the antiquity of which to me is unknown," Stow wrote in 1596—was a pulpit-cross, raised on three steps, at the northeast angle of the choir, where an outdoor sermon was preached each week and where ecclesiastical matters were settled or church decisions and sometimes others made known.

April 20, 1662, since because of rain and wind he could "by no means get a boat or a coach to carry" him to Whitehall he "staid at Paul's, where the Judges did all meet, and heard a sermon, it being the first Sunday of the term." He thought it "a very poor sermon," hardly worth going out into the "rain, and the wind [which were] against me."

Again, February 28, 1664, he "walked to Paul's; and by chance it was an extraordinary day for the Readers of the Inns of Court and all the Students to come to church, it being an old ceremony not used these twenty-five years, upon the first Sunday in Lent. Abundance there was of Students, more than there was room to seat but upon forms, and the Church mighty full. One Hawkins preached, (an Oxford man) a good sermon. . . . Both before and after sermon I was most impatiently troubled at the Quire, the worst that ever I heard."

During the Fire, on Tuesday September 4, 1666, Pepys could say, as the worst, no more than "Paul's is burning." After the Fire, its destruction centered for him at the desolation of the town.

On the seventh, Friday, he was up at five o'clock. He went "by water to Paul's Wharf" a mile up the Thames from the Tower, and then walked a quarter of a mile north to the Cathedral. He saw "all the towne burned, and a miserable sight of Paul's church, with all the roof fallen, and the body of the quire fallen into [the crypt]; Paul's school also, . . . my father's house, and the church" of St. Bride's. Evils were piling up. All men's minds were full of distractions upon this fire, of discontents, and of care. . . . The "militia is in arms every where." The English fleet had suffered "most unhappily by foule weather," and was "in very bad condition as to stores, victuals, and men. . . . The churches are set open to receive poor people" And enemies were plotting; none could be sure who was the enemy. Literally, awake and asleep. Pepys was haunted.

Out of the shock, London found its way. Time brought balance. Plans for rebuilding London—never carried out—were drawn up. In August two years later, St. Paul's steeple was pulled down, "with . . . ease: it is said that . . . another church is to be begun this year in the room thereof." That other church was not begun until

53

June 21, 1675. Evelyn wrote that the Sunday, eighteen years later, December 5, 1697, "was the first Sunday that St. Paul's had had service performed in it since it was burned in 1668."

The church Pepys knew was Old St. Paul's, in Pepys's time almost 600 years old, with earlier churches dimly seen before the Conquest. The Old St. Paul's was longer than any church in England is today; "most wonderful for length." Stow wrote "The height of the steeple was five hundred and twenty feet . . .; the length of the whole church is two hundred and forty tailor's yards, which make seven hundred and twenty feet; the breadth thereof is one hundred and thirty feet, and the height of the body of that church is one hundred and fifty feet."

William the Conquerer had part in its building (the Cathedral "burned with fire" the year of his death) and so did his sons and the three Edwards, and Richard II to honour Anne his wife, and Henry VI, Henry VII, and other kings. Sir Thomas More and John Donne and John Colet were deans of St. Paul's in the 1500's. Colet in 1512 built and endowed a school for 153 "poor men's children to be taught free." That was Pepys's school.

St. Paul's fell into poor condition. In Shakespeare's time and into the Commonwealth, the nave was a popular promenade, the "Paul's Walk" of Henry IV, and a market, and a place for businessmen to meet, and for gossiping. Charles I made Inigo Jones the architect to restore the Cathedral and built a splendid Ionic portico. The Commonwealth stopped all that: St. Paul's was an abomination. John Evelyn wrote from London on December 18, 1648: "in . . . Paul's Church . . . they [Commonwealth soldiers] had made stables for their horses, making plentiful fire with the seats." The Restoration again turned the wheel of fortune. Charles II appointed a Royal Commission for restoring and rebuilding St. Paul's.

Only a week before the Cathedral was burned, John Evelyn who was one of the three Royal surveyors, and Sir Christopher Wren, and the bishop of London, and "several expert workmen," went with others "to survey the general decays of that ancient and venerable church, and to set down in writing the particulars of what was fit to be done, with the charge thereof." (Evelyn, August 27, 1666). Repairs began, unhurriedly, for some of the Commission wanted a wholly new church and some wanted strengthening of walls and much rebuildings.

* * * * * *

Old St. Paul's for six hundred years dominated London. It stood

54

out, on a hill, high above other buildings, centering the general view of London from any compass-point by its size and bulk and position. About it in 1666 were the lesser belfries and spires and steeples of 109 City churches, built to the glory of God. Every day their bells set up a great clamor, though the old nursery rhymes seemed to show that Londoners found it a friendly uproar. "Bow bells and all the bells in all the Churches as we went home were aringing," Pepys wrote. But the burning of 89 City churches in the Great Fire took from him for years much of the sound of bells.

THE PLAGUE

The year 1665 was the year of the Great Plague. On the Continent, for more than a year it had been an ominous background to England, getting closer and darker and more real. The spring of 1665 it came to the coast towns and spread into the country, and then was in London. June 10, Pepys wrote that the Plague was nearby, at his "good friend and neighbor's, Dr. Burnett, in Fanchurch Street." He finished his letters at the office that night, and went home to bed much "troubled at the sicknesse ... and particularly how to put my things and estate in order, in case it should please God to call me away, which God dispose of to his glory!" That was only the day after he felt so much "joy of the good newes ... of our victory over the Dutch" that he went out to his tailor's, and, though for a long time he had been wearing only black, bought a suit of colored silk.

Through the summer and early fall, the Plague increased. In London, the first week of June 267 died of it; the week of September 19, the height of the Plague after the heat of summer, 7,165 died. That year, 70,000 died in a city of about 450,000. Most who could got away from London. July 5 Pepys sent his wife to Woolwich, where she stayed until January 6. The texture of government and amusements and church-going and business and other usual ways of London changed. The Court shifted to Hampton Court, then to Salisbury, and in September to Oxford. Parliament met in Oxford. The City officials stayed and worked with energy and sense, and the Navy Office worked on, busy under the drive of the increasing war. Lincoln's Inn locked its gates to all but its few students still in London, among them William Penn, and to some "persons of Quality." All theatres, fairs, gardens, and other places of assembly were closed. Most churches, too, were closed except for burials, and it is said many of the parishes were left empty of ministers. All building, and manufacturing, and shipping on the Thames, and all inland trade out of London stopped. An "innumerable multitude" of shopmen, clerks, office people, and servants, especially house servants, flooded out over London—"turned off, and left friendless and helpless," penniless, "without habitation." A "dismal article," a contemporary called it.

Pepys worked on in London through the summer and the fall. As the Plague increased, he saw in Drury Lane doors marked with a red cross a foot square and chalked with "Lord have mercy upon us." "Which was a sad sight to me." He saw, too, by day in Drury Lane corpses taken away in open carts, the "dead-carts." Earlier in the Plague, the carts had passed only at night. Taverns where he had dined one day he found closed the next; "poor Payne, my waiter, hath buried a child, and is dying himself." Will Hewer's father died of the Plague in September. Pepys's doctor died the third of August.

"It struck me very deep this afternoon," he wrote on June 17, that "going with a hackney coach . . . down Holborne, the coachman I found to drive easily and easily [slower and slower], at last [the coach] stood still, and [the coachman got] down [from his seat] hardly able to stand, and told me that he was suddenly struck very sicke, and almost blind, he could not see; so I 'light and went into another coach, with a sad heart for the poor man and trouble for myself, lest he should have been struck with the Plague; . . . but God have mercy upon us all!"

Pepys tells that one day, the third of August, in a narrow country lane, some young gentlemen were passing a coach which had the curtains drawn close, and one of "our gallants . . . being a young man, and believing there might be some lady in it that would not be seen . . . thrust his head out of his into her coach." He saw "somebody look very ill, and in a sick dress," and she "stunk mightily": a tale for a Medieval Morality.

The smell of the Plague hung over the City. To lessen it, sea-coal fires were lighted in many streets "about every twelfth door." At Moorefields and Finnsbury Fields and other open spaces outside the walls and in churchyards, fires burned by the pits where the dead were buried, tightly wrapped, at least six feet down. Burial usually was at night in the light of the pit-fires. Streets were empty then, and contamination less likely. One day, June 7, 1665, "the hottest day that ever I felt in my life," Pepys was "put . . . into an ill conception of myself and my smell, so that I was forced to buy some roll-tobacco to smell to and chaw, which took away the apprehension." In the summer Pepys had not dared to wear a periwig he had bought in Westminster, where the sickness had been strong; and he wondered whether anyone ever again would wear a wig since the hair might have been cut from someone who had died of the Plague. He did wear his periwig in September, and after.

Remedies were unending and fantastic. Of one remedy a doctor wrote in August: "many weare amulets made of the poison of a toad ... I may ... get the true preparation of it and send you." He wrote again: "Freind, get a piece of angell gold [a gold coin stamped with the archangel Michael slaying the dragon], if you can Eliz, coine (it is the best) ... and keepe it allways in your mouth when you walke out or any sicke persons come to you; you will find strange effects of it for good ... as I have done." You were to let it lie "betweene your cheeke and gumms, and so turning it sometime on one side, sometimes on the other." There were hundreds of other such phantasies. But they "will not do the worke of stopping God's hand; nothing but repentence will do that ... God is resolved to staine the pride of all glory ... I hear [that] ... above 7 score doctors, apothecarys, and surgeons are dead of this distemper."

The Plague brought lawlessness. In London at night and often in the daytime, Pepys carried "a very neat cane" against street dogs and ruffians. And one August night in the country near Woolwich, he was troubled when he had to walk past Coombe farm, "a single house, all alone from the towne." In the dark at ten o'clock he was fearful of the dogs at the farm, and more of the "rogues by the way," but most "because of the plague which is there." At Coombe farm, 21 had died of the Plague. The next morning as he walked past Coombe farm on his way to Greenwich, he saw a coffin with a plague corpse in it lying on the open ground of the farm; "the parish," he wrote, "having not appointed any body to bury it; but only set a watch there day and night, that nobody should go thither or come thence." Pepys thought that a most cruel thing.

In London, too, at any house where the Plague came, constant watch was set "to keep the people in, the plague making us cruel, as doggs, one to another." Yet he saw that people showed vast foolishness unless they were restrained. The Justices of the Peace had to be "doing something for the keeping of the Plague from growing. Lord! to consider the madness of the people of the town [Greenwich, where he met with the Justices], who will (because they are forbidden) come in crowds along with the dead corps to see them buried."

All around Pepys London was shaken and changed, and full of fear. So was Pepys's life—his habits, and his thoughts and moods.

Through the summer his life had a curious mixing. He was intensely absorbed at the Navy Office. He was delighted beyond his telling by the English victory at sea in June. He was happy at home. Yet the Plague pressed upon him. In a heavy mood, he put his affairs in order, "the season growing so sickly, that it is to be feared [no] man can escape having a share with others," and he prayed the good Lord God bless him and save him from death or fit him to receive it. All one night in early July he was much troubled in his sleep with dreams of Jack Cole, his old schoolfellow, "lately dead, who was born at the same time with me, and we reckoned our fortunes pretty equal. God fit me for his condition."

Yet at the end of July he was largely happy again. August 7, he wrote Lord Sandwich, who was with the fleet, that he felt "an excess of satisfaction" at the marriage, the week before, of Lord Sandwich's daughter, Lady Jemima—intelligent, merry, affectionate, unspoiled, for years quite Pepys's favorite—with Philip Carteret, the son of Sir George, Treasurer of the Navy; both very young—she seventeen, he twenty-four—and to Pepys delightful in their shyness and simplicity. They quite deserved one another, he was sure. Pepys had been negotiator and tutor in the marriage. "I am mightily, both with respect to myself and much more of my Lord's family, glad of this alliance."

So, during the summer of 1665, Pepys lived in the balance and counter-balance of the great fear which all the people had and the "greatest joy that ever I did [have] in my life." The time of the Plague was horrible to him beyond imagining, yet at the height of it in September 1665, he was entirely delighted by his ride up the hill to the heath and over the cart-tracks in Colonel Blunt's new chariot made with springs.

At the end of December, free from the weight of the year and feeling as he often did only the intensity of the present, he wrote (callously, it must be said, if with truth): "I have never lived so merrily . . . as I have done this plague time." Much had happened which satisfied him. The wedding seemed all happiness. His part in it had brought him "abundance of joy . . . honor . . . pleasant journeys, and brave entertainment . . . without cost of money." He had, besides, "raised [his] estate from £1300 in this year to £4400." He had become Treasurer for Tangiers, and Surveyor of the Victuals at 300 pounds a year. He had had much good talk and good company, as he says, and had been with those who sang well and those whose learning he enjoyed. "It is true we have gone through great melancholy because of the great plague," he wrote in December, "and I put to great charge by it," and the war was heavy on him, and Parliament was opposing what he was sure was best ("money [must] be got for the Navy, else we must shut up shop"), and "many of such as I know very well, [are] dead." Yet by the end of 1665 the Plague was almost over, and his wife and the maids, and his clerks—his "other family"— were back home in London. To his "great joy the town fills apace, and shops begin to open again. Pray God continue the plague decrease," for all public matters and private matters, too, "go to rack" while government, trade, the Court, and the usual structures of the City were upset. But health and usual ways were coming back.

* * * * * *

To William Penn, the summer was an intense and haunted time. Though he was often with his father on the Royal Charles and went on at Lincoln's Inn (which between May 8 and October 23 was in session only three weeks), he felt the growing horror of the Plague around him in London. Twelve years afterward, the sobering experience of the year still was strong and recurring. In his *Travails* (1677) he told that at "the time of the Great Plague in London" the Lord gave him "the deep sense of the Vanity of this World." To the Lord, in that extremity he made "Mournful and bitter cries . . . that he should show me his own way of Life and Salvation"; and he resolved "to follow him whatever reproaches or sufferings should attend."

THE GREAT FIRE

The Fire of 1666 is the greatest calamity London had until the Blitz. It lasted four and a half days; from, say, early Sunday morning, September 2, through Monday, Tuesday, Wednesday, and into Thursday, September 6. It destroyed 373 acres, four-fifths of the City, where about 300,000 people lived. It burned 13,200 buildings—houses, shops, churches, public buildings such as Gresham's Exchange, part of London Bridge, St. Paul's, 87 City churches, and 44 out of 51 Company Halls, among them Cloth-workers' Hall, 200 yards northwest of Pepys's house. In a rough oblong, for 1½ miles from the Tower to the Temple, it burned east and west along the Thames, and for ½ mile north from the Thames to Smithfield. These are the figures reported by City Surveyors soon after the Fire. It is said not more than a dozen people died in the Fire.

The Fire burned medieval London north of the Thames, Shakespeare's London—the streets and the churches and shops and taverns and theatres he wrote of, and the guild halls, and the houses of nobles and great merchants and of the middle class and the very poor. It ended the old City bounded by walls and gates, the London Henry V and Elizabeth and even Chaucer had known, a London much of which had lasted into the time of Pepys.

Pepys saw the Fire first when Jane Birch, one of the maids, woke him and his wife about three Sunday morning, to tell of a great fire in the City. He looked at it from Jane's window and thought it a faroff negligible little blaze, and went to sleep again.

Sunday morning, about seven, as he was dressing he looked again at the fire, from his window. It seemed not so much, and it was farther off. By and by Jane came. She told him she had heard "that above 300 houses had been burned down to-night by the fire we saw, and that it is now burning down all Fish-street by London Bridge." To test the rumor he walked to the Tower and climbed

61

"upon one of the high places," the Lieutenant of the Tower's little son going with him. In the southwest, along the river, was an "infinite great fire." The summer had been very dry and September 2 was a windy day. "So I down to the water-side, and there got a boat and through bridge, and there saw a lamentable fire . . . rage every way." After about an hour he went on up the Thames to tell the King and the Duke of York what he had seen; "and . . . that unless his Majesty did command houses to be pulled down nothing could stop the fire."

At noon he was home. After dinner he walked to St. Paul's, through "streets full of nothing but people and horses and carts loaden with goods, ready to run over one another." Much later, when it was dark, he began packing his own goods, for the fire was increasing and spreading eastward, and by moonlight, "it being brave dry, and moonshine, and warm weather," he took much of them into the garden, put his money and iron chests in the cellar, and "got my bags of gold into my office, ready to carry away, and my chief papers of accounts also there." These papers he buried Tuesday night in the garden. All Sunday night, "So much noise being in my house, taking down of goods [there was no] sleep . . . to me nor my poor wife."

At four the next morning, a cart sent by Lady Batten came "to carry away all my money, and plate, and best things," the Diary among them, to Sir W. Rider's at Bethnal Green. Pepys, wearing his nightgown, rode in the cart. Bethnal Green was safe open country two miles or less north and east of Seething Lane.

He was home before noon, though people running and riding and many carts crowded all highways and streets. The rest of the day and most of the night, he and his wife and the servants kept on packing, until the house was bare of even a spoon. John Tooker found for Pepys that afternoon a lighter, a river-barge, to take away the goods. Everybody ("myself one") carried them to the lighter, above Tower Wharf. John Tooker, Pepys had brought into the Commissioners' office a year or so before "to serve us as a husband to see goods timely shipped off . . to the Fleet." He was, that is, a manager of supplies; Pepys thought an excellent one— "a very painful poor man as ever I knew." Late that night Pepys and his wife fed upon the remains of their yesterday's dinner, without fire or dishes, and lay down for a little on quilts in his office.

Tuesday, the fourth, he worked from daybreak until after noon carrying the last of his goods to the lighter, was at his office awhile, walked into the panic of Tower Street, buried some Naval papers in his garden, ate mutton "without any napkin or anything," walked again on Tower Street, heard explosions as houses east of him were blown up, and after sunset from his garden watched the fire, which to him was so horrible it seemed enough to put him out of his wits. He and his wife again lay down upon Will Hewer's quilts in the office, Pepys being very weary, and sore in his feet.

About two the next morning, Wednesday, his wife woke him to tell him "new cryes of fire" were coming from All Hallows Barking Church, which was a quarter of a mile to the south, at the bottom of Seething Lane. By three o'clock, being sure that his home and all the Naval Office and St. Olave's and everything else near would soon be burning he took his wife, Hewer, Jane, and his 2,350 pounds by boat down the river to Woolwich past the burning town: "but, Lord! what a sad sight it was by moone-light to see the whole City amost on fire."

At seven, daylight, he was home again, alone; and as his end of the Lane seemed not in danger he went to the other end, the south, where at three o'clock that morning All Hallows was about to go. He found the fire there almost put out "by the blowing up of houses" and by workmen from the King's navy yards. Only the clock-face ["the dyall"] and part of the porch had been burned. The fire had been stopped north and south and west within one street of his house.

Pepys climbed the tower of All Hallows to see what London was like after the three days. From the tower he looked out over the ruined city, south to the Thames, and north toward Smithfield, and west to the Temple and Whitehall. He tells it this way: "I up to the top of Barking steeple, and there saw the saddest sight of desolation that I ever saw; every where great fires, oyle-cellars, and brimstone, and other things burning. I became afeard to stay there long, and therefore down again as fast as I could, the fire being spread as far as I could see it. . . . Clothworkers' Hall, one street north of the Navy Office, stayed on fire these three days and nights in one body of flame, it being the cellar full of oyle."

Late Thursday night the Fire was over. London started getting out a little from the dark mood—from the destructions and un-certainty of the Fire; from the breaking down of government routine and individual habits; from the wrenching of life into dangers and discomforts. London started getting back to disciplined relations. Thursday morning, September 6, Pepys realized (it seems, suddenly), that he was "all in dirt from top to bottom," and so he tried "to shift" himself—to wash and to change his shirt, but no shop in Westminster was open, and he "could not . . . buy a shirt" or be shaved. Finally, he did get trimmed at the Swan Tavern, where he often went.

The next day, Friday, September 7, he was up at five and began trying to get on with his usual work. To find out exactly what had happened, he walked into the center of London: "all the towne burned, and a miserable sight of Paul's church, with all the roofs fallen, and the body of the quire fallen" into the crypt; "Paul's school [his old school] also [was burned, and] Ludgate, and Fleet-street, my father's house, and the church [St. Bride's, where he had been christened], and a good part of the Temple." He went along the Strand, east of the burnings, to the lodging of John Creed, whom Pepys knew in the Admiralty and in the Tangier Commission and the Royal Society. Pepys "borrowed a shirt of him and washed." Then, at Sir William Coventry's chambers in St. James's Palace, he talked a long time with Sir William, the Duke of York's secretary, about the Fire and the Dutch War. Sir William hoped the fire would not bring riots and other lawlessness, or wild accusations against the Catholics, the French, the Dutch, or the Sectarians. Before noon, back at Seething Lane, Pepys gave "orders for [his] house to be made clean." Then, he went to his wife at Woolwich, dined there, came back to London, and spent the evening at Sir William Batten's talking of reestablishing businesses in the City; and he slept at Sir William Penn's, "without curtains or hangings," in "a naked bed."

Saturday, September 8, he and officers at the Admiralty went to work again. They met early at "Sir W. Coventry's chamber [in St. James's Palace], and there did what business we can, without any books." (Some books and records, Pepys had sent away; some he had buried in the Navy Office garden.) "Our discourse, as every thing else was confused." After dinner "to Bednall Green by coach, and fetched away my journall-book to enter for five days past. . . . To the office and late writing letters." At last, at Sir William Penn's, with difficulty, he slept.

Sunday morning, September 9, a week after the start of the Fire, he did not, it seems, go to his office. He went alone to St. Olave's. The "parson made a melancholy but good sermon; and many and most in the church cried, specially the women. The church mighty full; but few of fashion, and most strangers." After church he "walked to Bednall Green, and there dined well," at noon. "Thence home, and to church again," where the Dean of Rochester "preached . . . but, methinks, a bad, poor sermon, though proper

64

for the time." After that, he wrote in his journal. Late in the afternoon, it rained "which it hath not done a great while." He was troubled because of homeless people and their belongings, "though it is good for the fyre. Anon to Sir W. Pen's to bed, and made my boy Tom to read me asleep."

Within a week, matters at the office were settling into routine of a sort. He had his books again. They all in the office were driven hard by crowding work. On September 15, while his clerks were busy, he "wrote near thirty letters and orders with [his] owne hand. At it till eleven at night." And he thought it "strange to see how clear my head was, being eased of all the matter of these letters whereas one would think that I should have been dazed." The next day, Sunday, just two weeks after the start of the Fire, he was at "the office, whither also all my people . . . busy all the morning"; and "after dinner . . . to my office again, and there till almost midnight and my people with me, and then home, my head mightily akeing about our accounts."

At home, too, the old security was being established, for his wife was with him and the house was getting toward what it had been. He wrote, September 15, when he was most beset by business, that to his "great satisfaction" the workmen had "put up [his] beds and hangings" and that he did "find to [his] infinite joy many rooms clean." So he and his wife were able to sleep in their "own chamber again."

Getting his home as it had been took time and much work. It had been filthy from roof to cellar; most of the glass had been broken from the windows by explosions, and the furnishings had all been to Deptford and back or to Bethnal Green. Pepys and the repairmen worked without rest; for a week he did not take time to shave ("Lord! how ugly I was . . .!"). Though the Fire had ended September 6 his house was not clean until September 22; on the seventeenth, Pepys saw "much fire being still in" the City. But on September 22, his whole house was, he wrote, "so clean as I never saw it, or any other house in my life. . . . My glazier, indeed, is so full of worke that I cannot get him to come to perfect my house." The glazier did put in the windows a week later, September 28. Even with his broken windows, Pepys wrote a second time, September 22, that he found his "house in the best condition that ever I knew it," and, the next day, "my house being so clean makes me mightily pleased."

Ten days before his house was all clean, he had brought home his "gold" and many of his goods. He, "with Balty [his brother-in-law] and labourers from Deptford," on September 13, "did get [his] goods housed well at home . . . saving pictures and fine things" which he planned to "bring . . . when [his home would be] fit to receive them." That night he and his wife went "to bed in [their] house, the first time." They slept in his study "upon the ground" [on the floor]—yet to their "exceeding satisfaction." Pepys, however, was "troubled . . . to see all [his] goods lie up and down the house in a bad condition, and strange workmen going to and fro [who] might take what they would almost." And in early September at his office he had "infinite of business . . . to be done on a sudden." But his goods did get placed and he found at the end of the month that by repairs (which cost him about £20), and a few buyings, "every thing [would be] in as good condition as ever before the fire." Almost all his goods were a little harmed, but only a little: the gilt frames of some pictures were hurt and the gilding on some of his books. His bookbinder came September 28, "to gild the backs of my books" and the glazier, when he had finished with the windows, replaced the glass of Pepys's "book-presses"—the book-cases now in the Pepys Library at Cambridge.

Pepys got back to his gaieties. Friday, ten weeks from the Fire (November, 1666), after he had done "a good deale of business," he did "dress himself very fine" (he had bought a new vest) and he and his wife and eight or ten others went about five o'clock to pretty Mrs. Pierce's. There they danced, and he and Mrs. Knipp sang, "and Captain Downing (who loves and understands musique) would . . . have my song 'Beauty, retire'." Captain Downing praised the song—"and I know it is good in its kind." As they were dancing later, they were frightened by a great fire's breaking out at White-hall. "The whole town [was] in an alarme. Drums beat and trumpets, and guards every where spread, running up and down in the street." They heard houses blown up. Pepys was anxious about his own house. But the fire lessened; they supped, danced "another dance or two," and "merrily parted, and home." A few of them sat at cards with Pepys "till two in the morning, . . . drinking lamb's wool"—ale mixed with sugar, nutmeg, and the pulp of roasted apples.

Through early fall, the War and the clearing up of his house used his time to the limit, yet in these months the mood of the fire kept coming strongly back. September 7 he wrote: "but still both sleeping and waking had a fear of fire in my heart"; on the fifteenth, "much terrified in the nights now-a-days with dreams of fire, and falling down of houses"; on September 25, "all night still

mightily troubled in my sleepe with fire and houses pulling down";
and on September 27, "A very furious blowing night all the night;
and my mind still mightily perplexed with dreams, and burning
the rest of the town; and waking in much pain for the fleete."

Though the dreams faded, for the next months he was greatly
troubled. His own affairs went well. He had "above 620l."; he loved
his wife and was proud of her; his song "Beauty, Retire," was being
written, if slowly; he thought well of himself and of his position,
and he had a household of five servants, and a fine house, and he
carried ahead the office affairs. These and much else were quite—
or almost—to his satisfaction. Yet for months that winter he was
greatly troubled: by the disasters of the Dutch War, and Den-
mark's declaration of war, and the rising in Scotland, and the
war-threat by France; by the breaking down of discipline in the
Navy and the low state of the fleet ("Our losses both in reputation
and ships have been greater ... than ... in all ages past"); by the
"great folly in Parliament" and its antagonism to the Navy and to
the Duke of York, and its failure to make needed grants; by the
neglect and extravagance and triviality of the Court, and his "grief
... that the King does not look after his business himself, it
being ... not yet too late if he would apply himself ... to save all
and conquer the Dutch"; by the loss to London in capital money
(there was no insurance) and in rents (600,000 pounds for the year)
and in trade; and by talk that the City would never be rebuilt. But
what disturbed him most was a strong, pervasive, uncentered fear
that somehow ruin would strike the whole kingdom (December 31,
1666). He did "foresee great unhappiness coming upon us"—possibly "an invasion the next year," possibly "risings," riots in the
City, fires, "massacres," horrors he could not see the outlines of.
He found "all people mightily at a loss what to expect, but confusion and fears in every man's head and heart." All men "fear
the event will be bad." Like the rest of London, he was living in the
shock of the past months.

Six years earlier he had seen "the City from one end to the other
with a glory about it, so high was the light of the bonfires, ... and
the bells rang everywhere" as Charles II came home.

* * * * * *

Pepys has written far and away the best account there is of the
Fire. It is much quoted and much worth quoting. It is alive, for
Pepys saw and felt what he told, and he could tell it. He catches
details of what the Fire meant to someone who was watching his

home burn into nothing; and he gives, too, the rush and the mass and power of the Fire, its inescapability:

Before noon, Sunday, the first day of the Fire, Pepys watched from a boat the fire sweeping along the waterfront. He wrote: "Everybody endeavouring to remove their goods, and flinging into the river or bringing them into lighters that lay off; poor people staying in their houses . . . till the very fire touched them, and then running into boats, or clambering from one pair of stairs by the water-side to another. And among other things, the poor pigeons, I perceive, were loth to leave their houses, but hovered about the windows and balconys till they were, some of them burned, their wings, and fell down. Having staid, and in an hour's time seen the fire rage every way, . . . the wind mighty high and driving it into the City; and every thing, after so long a drought, proving combustible, even the very stones of churches, . . .: I to White Hall."

Before sunset the same day, the fire "still increasing, and the wind great," Pepys with his wife and three others again watched the fire from a boat in the river. "So near the fire as we could for smoke; and all over the Thames, with one's face in the wind, you were almost burned with a shower of fire-drops. This is very true; so as houses were burned by these drops and flakes of fire, three or four, nay, five or six houses, one from another. When we could endure no more upon the water, we to a little ale-house on the Bankside, over against the Three Cranes, and there staid till it was dark almost, and saw the fire grow; and, as it grew darker, appeared more and more, and in corners and upon steeples, and between churches and houses, as far as we could see up the hill of the City, in a most horrid malicious bloody flame, not like the fine flame of an ordinary fire... We staid till, it being darkish, we saw the fire as only one entire arch of fire ... in a bow up the hill for an arch of above a mile long: it made me weep to see it. The churches, houses, and all on fire and flaming at once; and a horrid noise the flames made, and the cracking of houses at their ruine. So home with a sad heart."

PRICES

I

The Diary is not an expense account. Usually Pepys told price only when price was part of his interest. The cost of a silk coat was satisfying or it was an alarming extravagance, and so he told its cost; a telescope for looking at the moon was worth the money; the 2 shillings, 1 pence he had paid for a pound of cherries in June, when he "walked in the fields . . . and sang [near] Old Ford, a town by Bow," was part of the pleasant memory.

Service was cheap. At Axe Yard, Pepys paid Jane one pound a year and gave her food and clothing and a room, and she was in the household. His salary at the Exchequer in 1657 was 50 pounds a year. He and his wife and Jane lived on a pound a week; and they had their pleasures and he, somehow, saved a little. Elizabeth Pepys worked hard at housework, and watched accounts with care. Pepys, in 1659, had 40 pounds lent out to his uncle Robert Pepys, who was wealthy enough to leave to Pepys's father a small estate at Brampton, 60 miles north of London, and an uncertain 80 pounds a year, and long litigation. But all that came after Pepys was at Seething Lane. At Axe Yard, and before, they lived meagerly.

Jane Wayneman, the maid, justifies a digression. She is worth knowing—innocent, dreamy, at times stubborn, happy, hardworking, almost a child, able and expected it seems to do everything, and devoted to her two brothers, who, Pepys thought, were likely to end on the gallows. The Diary touches her in, convincingly. One morning, for some negligence, Pepys "took a broom and basted her till she cried extremely" (December 1, 1660); and one night while he lay in bed "reading myself asleep, . . . the wench sat mending my breeches by my bedside": a good interior by candlelight. Another night he was "very ill—I think with eating and drinking too much"—and had to call Jane, "who pleased my

wife and I in her running up and down so innocently in her smock"
(December 27, 1660). When Pepys went out at night on the un-
lighted streets, she carried a lantern, and she combed his hair
before he went to sleep, and when a great washing of clothes was
to be done she started it at two in the morning. Pepys records that
"Sir W. Pen did tell me . . . of my Jane's cutting off a carpenter's
long mustacho, and how the fellow cried" (September 14, 1662):
a matter astonishing and forever a teasing mystery, hidden and
absurd. When for two or three days she was lame, they, naturally,
could not "tell what to do for want of her." Jane was with Pepys
until February, 1663, three years. He "could hardly forbear shed-
ding tears" when she left. After that she is in the dark outside the
Diary, except once, when six months later she came to Pepys's
office and for two hours begged him to employ her brother Will
again, whom Pepys in early July had "sent . . . going," or at least
find him a place at sea. "The poor girl cried all the time she was
with me, and would not go from me . . . but receive him I will not,
nor give him anything" (July 28, 1663).

Service was cheap, and so were simple foods—common vegetables and fruits (for the most part disregarded in the Diary),
common cheese, coarse bread, many sorts of fresh fish, dried cod,
pigs' feet, and neat's foot, and sheep's trotters, and calves' head,
beef heart, and other such anatomical parts, and small beer and
ale. Quite out of this simple range was Pepys's first Christmas
dinner as Clerk of the Acts: "a good shoulder of mutton and a
chicken." So was a pullet stewed for himself and his wife, and his
buying "a leg of beef, a good one, for six pence, and my wife says
is worth my money." He went "all alone to the Black Spread Eagle
in Bride Lane, and there had a chopp of veale and some bread,
cheese, and beer, cost me a shilling to my dinner" (September 7,
1663). While he was at Axe Yard, he could not pay for such food.

Fine clothes were expensive. Even common clothes—a black
stuff suit or a "mungo" dress of poor-grade reclaimed wool—were
not cheap. Pepys wore a black stuff suit at the Exchequer, though
his father was a tailor. When he was almost sure he would be
appointed Clerk of the Acts, he bought a "fine Camlett cloak, with
gold buttons, and a silk suit, which cost me much money, and
I pray God to make me able to pay for it." Camlett was silk and
wool. Even after his appointment, the cost of his clothing troubled
him. At the end of October, 1663, "to prepare my monthly account
. . . stayed till 10 or 11 o'clock at night, and to my great sorrow
find myself . . . worse . . . £ 55, or thereabouts; having made myself

70

a velvet cloake, two new cloth suits, black, plain both; a new shagg [cloth like plush] gowne, trimmed with gold buttons and twist, with a new hat, and silk tops for my legs, and many other things, being resolved hanceforward to go like myself." But in the later 1660's (October 30, 1664) he could afford "my new, fine, colored cloth suit, with my cloake lined with plush [Pepys seldom told colors], which is a dear and noble suit, costing me about £17." Eight months after that (June 1, 1665) "I put on my new silke camelott sute; the best that ever I wore in my life, the sute costing me above £24." His kid gloves were 2 shillings; one periwig was 3 pounds, another was 40 shillings. Against these can be set what he paid his surgeon: "Mr. Hollier . . . let me blood, about sixteen ounces, I being exceedingly full of blood. . . . I began to be sick; but lying upon my back I was presently well again, and did give him 5s for his pains" (May 4, 1662).

Books he bought often, usually from two booksellers, one in St. Paul's Churchyard, the other in Westminster Hall. He wrote of exchanging, discarding, rebinding, gilding his books, cataloguing them, and arranging them in his study. (Three thousand of his books are in the Pepys Library at Cambridge.) Sometimes he told the price he paid. An encyclopaedia, two volumes folio, was 38 shillings; a Latin dictionary in two volumes, a prize book for his old school, was 20 shillings; "Marcennus's book of musick . . . cost me £3/ 2; but is a very fine book." One day in December, 1663, the nineteenth, he made, extra, 2 or 3 pounds. So "to St. Paul's Churchyard, to my bookseller's. . . . I did here sit two or three hours calling for twenty books to lay this money out upon, and found myself at a great losse where to choose. . . . I could not tell whether to lay out my money for books of pleasure, as plays, which my nature was most earnest in. . . ." He looked at Chaucer, Stowe's *London,* Shakespeare, Jonson, Beaumont's plays, and other books. At last he chose Fuller's *Worthies,* letters of Ministers of James I and Charles I, *Hudibras,* "now in greatest fashion for drollery, though I cannot, I confess, see enough where the wit lies," and two or three small books "of good use or serious pleasure," one in French.

That was the third *Hudibras* Pepys bought. When the poem was first published, he paid one morning 2 shillings, 6 pence for a copy and at noon the same day sold it for 1 shilling, 6 pence; "it is so silly" (December 26, 1662). The second he bought six weeks later (February 6, 1663); for "all the world cries [it] to be the example of wit," and he was "resolved once again to read him, and see whether I can find it or no." He never told he found the wit. But one Sunday in July, 1668, "Mr. Butler, that wrote Hudibras," and other gentlemen dined with Pepys. It was "a good dinner and company that pleased me mightily, being all eminent men in their way. Spent all the afternoon in talk and mirth." Among these men were Hales the portrait painter, Samuel Cooper the miniaturist, Henry Harris the leading actor at Davenant's theatre, and Mr. Reeves who made perspective glasses.

Three times Pepys wrote of buying a perspective glass from Reeves. March 23, 1660, while he still was living in Axe Yard (The Diary was only three months old) "Young Reeve ... brought me a little perspective glass which I bought for my Lord, it cost me 8s." That was two weeks before he sailed for Holland, secretary to Lord Sandwich. August 13, 1664, "There comes ... Mr. Reeves [no longer young], with a microscope and scotoscope. For the first I did give him £5 10s., a great price, but a most curious bauble it is, and he says, as good, nay, the best he knows in England, and he makes the best in the world. The other he gives me, and is of value; and a curious curiosity it is to look objects in a darke room with." August 22, 1666, in the evening "home, and there find Reeves, and so up to look upon the stars, and do like my glasse [his telescope] very well, and did even with him for it and a little perspective and the Lanthorne that shows tricks, altogether costing me £9 5s. 0d." Six years before, he had paid 8s.

Pepys had written earlier of that telescope. Two weeks before he bought it, Mr. Reeves and he were on his roof trying to see the moon and Jupiter and Saturn, but the heavens proved cloudy and they lost their labor. The next night—"a mighty fine bright night"—they looked at the moon and Jupiter, though Pepys was very sleepy, till one in the morning, with a "twelve-foote glasse and another of six foote" which Mr. Reeves had brought with him that night. The "sights mighty pleasant, and one of the glasses I will buy, it being very useful" (August 7, 8, 1666).

II

The ratio of the pound which Pepys spent to the pound today is impossible to fix. The differences of 1660 and 1960 are ranged against exactness. Questions of comparisons can be asked: What would King Charles's gift of 4,000 pounds a year to Lord Sandwich mean today to a man with the relative income and position of Lord Sandwich? What relation had the cost of a loaf of bread, a pound of cheese, rent, working clothes in 1660 to a laborer's in-

come then? What was the farmer's income in proportion to the
great landowner's, and what demands were put on it, and what
food, clothing, equipment, and the rest did he expect to have?
Yet here to complicate comparison is the need to estimate the
immensely different kind and variety of things men three centuries
apart think they require. Twenty-five years ago it was said that
the pound Pepys spent might have been worth five times the
pound of 1935. In 1949, the pound changed from almost $5.00 in
the market to about $2.80; and differences between class demands
have narrowed since 1935. A magazine (*Atlantic,* April, 1957) gave
the value of the income dollar in 1900 as four times the value of
the income dollar today. Professor A. L. Rowse wrote in 1957 "we
must multiply by twenty for a modern equivalent" of the pound
of about 1600 (*S. Rev.,* Nov. 2, 1957).

Comparison is difficult. The worlds compared are materially far
apart. Yet it seems fair to say the pound of 1660 bought at least
fifteen times what the pound buys today, especially human labor
and goods in common use. But the structure of seventeenth century life—its demands and acceptances—comes in here to make
that ratio a very rough guide.

III

Pepys kept a clear account of his income and expenses. He
usually jotted rough notes of what he paid out each day, and of
what he did and thought. In the evenings, or on Sunday, fairly
soon, he sorted the items. Money items he put in his account; the
others he wrote out fully in the Diary.

However, in the manuscript of the Diary for 1668, Pepys in-
serted two sheaves of notes. One is 3 leaves (6 pages) of rough
jottings, for 9 days in April, when his eyes troubled him; the other
is 5 leaves, of jottings and full notes, for 13 days in June, when he
was traveling in the west of England. Evidently, he intended to
sift the items and write up those days in his Diary, for he left
blank pages in April and in June to hold them.

All through those notes are prices of services and of goods. The
notes for April give about 50 prices; those for June give even more.
This is nearly as many as are given in all the entries of some years.
The notes tell, too, what Pepys paid for usual things, routine to
him and to be sifted out into his expense account.

The rough notes for the 9 days in April (April 10 to April 19,
1668) give these prices among others:

73

	£	s.	d.
binding books		17	0
boat (according to distance)			
Tower Stairs to The Temple, 1½ miles		1	0
"by water, by moonshine, home," from			
The Temple, 1½ miles		1	0
short trips			6
coach			
Temple Bar, home, through St. James's Park			
[2 miles?]		2	6
Westminster, through Park, home, [3 miles?]		3	0
Westminster home		2	6
[Pepys paid coach-hire for his wife and maid from			
London to Brampton, 60 miles, June 14, 1663.]		35	0
"at the Quaker's," for two		3	6
after the play, for Mrs. Knipp and a young			
officer		16	6
[Will Hewer and he dined well at a cook's shop			
in Aldergate Street "upon roast beef"			19½
"drank all alone" at Harp-and-Ball			
Westminster. Pepys had gone to it since 1659.]			2
draft of ale			6
dues to Royal Society	1	6	0
oysters		1	0
theatre			
play, in the pit		2	0
play and oranges		2	6
a box at the Duke's Theatre		20	
[which "troubled" him (January 6, 1668)]			

In June the same year, 1668, Pepys went in his coach to the south
and west of England for a vacation trip. It lasted 13 days. Pepys
enjoyed it intensely.

With him after he left Brampton the eighth were his wife and
her maid, Deb Willett ("very pretty, and so grave as I never saw a
little thing in my life. Indeed I think her ... too good for my family,
and so well carriaged as I hardly ever saw"); Betty Turner, the very

young and delightful daughter of his good wealthy cousin, Jane Turner; Will Hewer, then twenty-five years old; and Mr. Murford, who had been a clerk with Pepys in the Exchequer, back when the Diary began. (The two probably rode horseback. On another journey, in October 1667, they had ridden beside the four-horse coach). Betty Turner carried a sparrow with her.

He went to Brampton, 60 miles north of London, to his father's, and then they circled away through Oxford, Salisbury and Stonehenge, Bath, Bristol, Bath again, and back to London. They left Brampton for Oxford early on Monday the eighth.

Oxford was "a very sweet place." On Tuesday and part of Wednesday, they all looked at a few colleges; Pepys went to "others very fine, alone with W. Hewer." He saw the libraries, the chapels, the Halls, the gardens, and the river. He heard some good music, had strawberries, walked in the fields, and found his lodgings excellent and cheap. "Oxford a mighty fine place."

On Wednesday after dark they came into Salisbury, having seen for most of the afternoon across the Plain the great spire of the cathedral. Salisbury was a brave town. "The river goes through every street." The cathedral was "most admirable; as big, I think, and handsomer than Westminster." He went to it three times one day, Thursday. Thursday morning, on horseback they all rode across Salisbury Plain to Stonehenge, the three women on pillions behind Will Hewer and Murford and the guide. Stonehenge, set in the quiet of the country, frightened Pepys. He found the great circle of stones "as prodigious as any tales I ever heard of them and worth going this journey to see. God knows what their use was!" Pepys gave a shepherd woman there 4 shillings for tending the horses at Stonehenge.

(Evelyn, in contrast, was not awed at Stonehenge; he was inquiring. Where had the great stones come from and how had they been brought? Were there 95 stones, as he counted, or 100? How hard were they? "[A]ll my strength with a hammer could not break a fragment; which hardness I impute to their so long exposure" July 22, 1654).

They left Salisbury Thursday the eleventh, at six, and went out over the wide plain. In the dark, "by a happy mistake" of their guide, they were carried out of their way. About ten they came "to a little inn, where he were fain to go into a room where a peddler was in bed, and made him rise; and there wife and I lay, and in a truckle-bed Betty Turner and Willett. But good beds." The next morning, "Up, finding our beds good, but lousy; which made us merry." Before dark they had come to Bath, Friday. Pepys was tired; "being weary, went to bed without supper; the rest supping." But first, typically, he did "step out . . . and saw the baths, with people in them." The baths were not so large as he had expected, "yet pleasant."

Bath, on hills above the Avon, was a pleasant town, clean, built most of stone, the streets narrow. They were all up at four o'clock the next day, Saturday, and each wrapped in a sheet, "were carried one after another, myself, and wife, and Betty Turner, Willett, and W. Hewer," in chairs to the Cross Bath, the one for the gentry, the rest being "full of the mixed sort, of good and bad." They had "designed to have done [finished their baths] before company came," but much company did come, "very fine ladies" and gentlemen. It was all "pretty enough only methinks it cannot be clean to go so many bodies together in the same water." Pepys found the water very hot. It also parboiled his feet, but he stayed above two hours in the water. Then in his sheet he was carried home to bed and lay sweating for an hour. "By and by comes musick to play to me, extraordinary good as ever I heard at London almost, or anywhere: 5s." They left Bath for the day at eleven, and at two were set down at the Horseshoe in Bristol.

Bristol, the second city in England, a great ship-building city, and wealthy, and crowded with inland and ocean commerce, Pepys thought "in every respect another London." That afternoon he walked alone "to see the quay, which is the most large and noble place," and to see a large ship being built, which would be a fine ship. When he came back to the Sun Inn, he found Deb and her Uncle Butts, "so like one of our sober, wealthy, London marchants." They all dined late and afterward they went walking to the quay and the ship and the Custom House, and Butts made "Pepys understand many things of the place, and led me through Marsh Street, where our girl was born. But, Lord! the joy there was among the old poor people of the place, to see Mrs. Willett's daughter." Pepys found the people of the town "pay him [Butts] great respect, and he the like to the meanest, which pleased me mightily." He brought them to his house and gave them "good entertainment of strawberries, a whole venison-pastry, cold . . . and above all Bristoll milk." Bristol had good food—turtle from the West Indies, Spanish wines, English venison, rum, and the strawberries of the west of England.

They drove back, a dozen miles to Bath, Saturday by moonlight. Pepys liked Bath. Sunday, which was the fifteenth, he "walked up

76

and down the town and saw many good streets, and very fair stone houses," and he went to morning service in the Abbey Church. He heard there a good organ, but a vain fellow preached a ridiculous affected sermon that made him angry. When the service was done he walked round the walls of the city, "the battlements all there," and came back to the inn. After dinner he and Mr. Butts went again to the Abbey, and again the silly fellow preached, and Pepys slept most of the sermon. Midafternoon, he took his "wife out and the girls" to see the beautiful Abbey (his third visit that day), and walked a little in the fields, and went then to supper. That evening the landlord, "a sober understanding man" came to him and gave him "a good account of the antiquities of this town and Wells. . . . But he is a Catholick." Monday morning, after a look into the baths, they all, Will Hewer included, started over the Downes for London, 120 miles, a journey of two and a half days by coach.

On this trip his spendings stand in part:

	£	s.	d.
June 8, Monday, 1668			
Brampton (left early A.M.)			
father's servants		14	0
road menders		2	0
on road to Oxford			
reckoning, noon		13	4
drink		1	0
church guide		1	0
reckoning, overnight		19	6
poor ("the poor . . . did stand at the coach to have something given them, as they do to all great persons" Oct. 9, 1667).		6	0
June 9, Tuesday			
Oxford (ar. 9 A.M. left 10 A.M. Wed.)			
guide to Oxford	1	2	6
barber		2	6
book *Stonage*		4	0
guides about Oxford	1	0	0
strawberries		1	2
music		5	0
dinner and servants, noon	1	0	6

	£	s.	d.
poor		1	0
"bottle of sack for landlord"		2	0
reckoning, overnight		13	0
poor		2	6

June 10, Wednesday

on road to Salisbury, all day (10 A.M. "till dark")

dinner		12	0
guide		3	6

June 11, Thursday

Salisbury (ar. dark Wed., left 6 P.M. Thurs.)

	£	s.	d.
Gorge Inn, reckoning ("exorbitant . . . I was mad")	2	5	6
poor		1	6
poor woman in streets		1	0
guide to Stonehenge		2	0
shepherd woman at Stonehenge for leading horses			4
washer woman		1	0
seamstress		3	0

June 12, Friday

on road to Bath

little inn on the Plain overnight, reckoning and servants		9	0
guide		2	0
dinner on road		10	0

June 13, Saturday

Bath (ar. "before night" Friday, left 11 A.M. Mon.)

chair-carriers		3	6
serjeant of the bath		10	0
music		5	0
trip to *Bristol* (Sat. 11 A.M. till 10 P.M.)			
shave		2	0

	£	s.	d.
cabin boy		2	0
dinner		7	6
reckoning		2	6

June 14, Sunday
Bath

	£	s.	d.
secton		1	0

June 15, Monday
Bath

	£	s.	d.
reckoning, 3 nights	1	8	6
servants		3	0
poor		1	0
boy to dive into King's bath		1	0
coach and horse to Bristol	1	1	6

June 15, 16, 17
on road to London

	£	s.	d.
reckoning, Monday night		14	4
servants		2	0
poor		1	0
reckoning, Tuesday noon		8	7
servants and poor		1	6
reckoning, Tuesday night		12	6
servants and poor		2	6

June 17, Wednesday

Colebrooke by noon; ... and there dined, and
fitted ourselves a little to go through London,
anon.... Thence pleasant way to London,
before night, and find all very well, to great
content....

PEPYS AND WILLIAM PENN

Four Portraits

Sir William Penn, William Penn, Pepys, and Elizabeth Pepys all were painted in 1666; all four paintings were thought good likenesses; all exist today, though one in an engraving; three of the persons painted were handsome, and Pepys by any test was notable—his face strong, individual, and intelligent.

Sir William Penn

Sir William was painted only once. For April 18, 1666, Pepys wrote: "I to Mr. Lilly's [Sir Peter Lely], the painter's; and there saw the heads, some finished, and all begun, of the Flaggmen [the Admirals] in the late great fight with the Duke of Yorke against the Dutch. The Duke of Yorke hath them done to hang in his chamber, and very finely they are done indeed."

There were thirteen portraits, among them Sir William's and Lord Sandwich's. These portraits now hang in the Painted Chamber at Greenwich.

Sir William's portrait shows him strongly built, handsome, young-looking though he was forty-five. He is a courtier in his dress—: loose-skirted uniform coat; full linen and lace at his wrists and about his neck; and across his chest from his right shoulder and low on his hip a wide embroidered baldric which holds his sword. He is backed by what seems the stone wall of a fortress and a stretch of ocean with a warship on it. His face is full, unlined, strong, well-featured; his eyes are large and marked with heavy brows and his chin is heavily rounded. A seaman who served under him wrote to William Penn: "Your late honored father was fair-haired, of a comely, round visage"; with which the portrait agrees. Sir William stands in easy command: a finished gentleman, a General of the Sea. The portrait does not suggest that Sir William, as a contemporary put it, liked a loose story and a bawdy song; or was

80

ever in the "mad, ridiculous, drunken humour" Pepys said he was; or could have been touched by almost religious seriousness; or had the force to win against Spaniards and Dutch; or hid the duplicity Pepys wrote was in him. Indeed, the portrait does not much show what Sir William was. It does not give the tang, the power, and the arresting strangeness of the person who is painted. It is conventional, for the occasion. Sir William is one of seventeen admirals placed and lighted but from the outside—by Lely's power to paint.

William Penn

The first portrait of William Penn, son of the Admiral, shows him at twenty-two, in armor. There are three such portraits, two copied from the third, the unidentified original. Of the three, two are in England and one is in the library of The Historical Society of Pennsylvania, in Philadelphia. The original, whichever it is, was painted by an unknown painter in the summer of 1666, after Penn had left Lincoln's Inn and gone to Dublin, to the court of the Lord Lieutenant the Duke of Ormonde. He volunteered there against the "rebel Irish," served on the expedition "to his no small reputation," and again in Dublin was eager to be a professional soldier. His father did not approve the choice. Penn had been educated for the civil service and diplomacy.

William Penn looks calmly from the picture, at ease, handsome, young, and elegant in his complete armor. The background is brown, an overall pattern of "ovals of medium brown with spandrels of a darker brown." Penn's lace cravat is wrapped twice or so about his neck and ends in full and graceful folds; the hair possibly a wig—a year later he wore "a great periwig"—is "dark brown," and after the fashion, is parted quite exactly and falls in thick waves upon his shoulders; his complexion is "pinkish pale"; his eyes are "dark brown," strongly set by heavy brows; and his mouth and nose—or so the painter forms them—are quite perfect in proportion and shape. (The phrases quoted are in a letter from The Historical Society of Pennsylvania.) His face is fairly full, unlined, and is very like his father's in features and expression, though the features are more finely turned and the expression more open, clear, and sensitive. It is a beautiful, young portrait. Penn in it is elegant and fine but not at all effeminate. He seems a "fortunate, cultivated, charming, almost ingenuous boy of twenty-two." Yet, his portrait, like his father's, does not record any incisions his action and feelings and thoughts had made on him. It does not suggest that in the past year he had known closely the Plague and in the next year would make a decision which changed every relation in his life.

Penn lived to be seventy-three; he went through many emotions and events, and his likenesses if not so many as his years are very many, from the 37-foot bronze in Philadelphia to a rather sharp-nosed, very plump, gnome-like little bust of him when he was old. Penn's likenesses record some strange effects from marching time.

Samuel Pepys

Pepys was dark, short, thickset, his expression animated and intelligent and attractive. One who saw him when he was forty-five said "he was a low, squat man." His portraits agree with that incomplete description—the only firsthand written description there is.

The Hayls portrait of him at thirty-three shows him "standing . . . seen to the elbow" against a "background plain dark brown. . . . The shadows are deep and of a reddish tone. . . . His face, turned three quarters to the left," is oval, full, smooth, with features well-shaped and definite. His eyes are large, "yellow-grey," spaced wide in his face, and are attractive and alert. "The eyebrows are brown and strongly defined, with a remarkable depression [of] skin between them." His forehead below his periwig is broad; his hair, "long dark brown." Nose and mouth and cheeks and chin are full. He is "wearing a yellow-brown loose (Indian) gown . . ., a plain white neckcloth loosely tied," and white cuffs. (The words quoted are in a letter from the National Portrait Gallery, London, where the portrait is.) "I . . . do almost break my neck looking over my shoulder to make the posture for him to work by," Pepys wrote. The gown, he "hired to be drawn in: an Indian gowne." Hayls thought the gown made good shadows in the folds. With his left hand, Pepys holds "the musique [of his own song Beauty Retire], which now pleases me mightily, it being painted true"—painted note for note. He looks out from the picture—pleasantly self-possessed, friendly, not arrogant or intense, quite the master of the situation: a young man of energy, good mind, good training, and good manners. Engravings of the portrait do not much suggest the mobility and force of life. The eyebrows and nose and mouth and chin make up almost the fixed and inexpressive roundings of a mask.

The progress of the portrait has pleasant though not large interest. At least its painting interested Pepys. From the first sitting, he liked it; "he will make me, I think, a very fine picture. He promises it shall be as good as my wife's" (March 17, 1666). Her picture was then almost finished, "and a beautiful picture it is, as almost I ever saw" (March 20, 1666). At his first sitting, Pepys had found the art greater than the likeness. He did not see just what was wrong, "but, whatever the matter is, I do not fancy that it has the ayre of my face, though it will be a very fine picture" (March 20). Then one day the likeness was there. The portrait "is become mighty like"; and so it stayed. To be sure, Pepys was for "putting out" the landscape background in favor of "a plain sky like my wife's picture, which will be very noble." Hayls, after trying counter-persuasion for keeping the landscape background, was "so civil as to say it should be altered," though, Pepys writes, "he do not like [the new background] so well." Two days later the landscape had been "done out, and only a heaven [plain dark brown] made in the roome of it." That change and the exact transcript of notes on the music sheet he held, made the portrait almost perfect to Pepys then and steadily afterward.

Pepys liked John Hayls. He found him a pleasant man, full of good talk, and tactful and urbane; a civil man, Pepys called him. In 1668 he had Hayls at dinner with four or five others, "all eminent men in their way." Hayls, he thought an admirable portrait painter. He had right ideas of pose and shadowings and background, and stood up for his opinions, but he could give in, as Pepys found, with grace. Before the portrait was painted, Pepys had been sure Hayls had "a very masterly hand" (February 14, 1666), and after it was finished and home, he "was very well satisfied in it," and "with great pleasure my wife and I hung [it] up." His portrait cost him "£ 14 for the picture, and 25s. for the frame" (May 16, 1666).

Pepys had his portrait painted at least nine times: from Savill's in 1661 to Verrio's in 1682. Two are in the National Gallery, two at Magdalene College, Cambridge, one at the Royal Society, and one, Verrio's group, at Christ Hospital.

Elizabeth Pepys

Three portraits were painted of Elizabeth Pepys. The first was painted by Savill, the winter of 1661. Savill was an undistinguished artist. His given name is not known, and his biography seems usually covered by "a painter in Cheapside." He began his painting of Elizabeth Pepys in December, (the thirteenth) at the time he was painting Pepys. Pepys never was enthusiastic about his own portrait or his wife's. At first, his own "do not please me, for I fear it will not be like me" (December 3), but he came to like it

83

"fairly." Later, both portraits "do not much displease me" (December 30). They pleased him better once they were in their frames (January 24, 1662), yet he was "of the opinion, that [my wife's] do much wrong her; but I will have it altered." He did (January 28). It came to be like her, he thought; but Savill "though a very honest man [was] silly as to . . . skill in shadows. . . . I was almost angry to hear him talk so simply." In late February (the twenty-second), he and his wife, with Savill, hung the two portraits in their dining room, which, he says, "comes now to appear very handsome with all my pictures." The next day, Sunday, "My cold being increased, I staid at home all day, pleasing myself with my dining-room, now graced with pictures, and reading of Dr. Fuller's *Worthys*." That evening he wrote: "This day by God's mercy I am 29 years of age, and in very good health, and like to live and get an estate; and if I have a heart to be contented, I think I may reckon myself as a happy man as any is in the world, for which God be praised. So to prayers and to bed."

Pepys liked the portraits well enough to have Savill paint a miniature of him. At the first sitting, February 20, 1662, it "pleaseth me well"; at the last sitting (April 14th) all he wrote was "I hope [it] will please me"; but three weeks later (May third), in a gold case, the miniature "pleases me exceedingly and my wife."

Hayls painted Elizabeth Pepys's portrait in February and March, 1666. Of her three portraits, Pepys liked this one best. It was "Mighty like her," "a very brave picture," a "beautiful picture . . . as almost I ever saw." Two years later, he took it back, and Hayls repainted the right hand. Hayls, Pepys wrote, was often "negligent" in painting a hand. Hayls had complained "that her nose cost him as much work as another's face, and he hath done it finely indeed" (March 3, 1666).

Pepys, all through, had two tests for a portrait. He says, acutely, (August 21, 1668) that Lely's portraits at Hampton Court of the Maids of Honor are "good, but not like," and his wife's when Hayls had "mended" the hand was "very like . . . and a brave work." Savill's did not quite have either good painting or a likeness. Cooper's was "very fine," "most admirable," "a noble picture, but yet I think not so like as Halse's is" (July 18, 1668).

Hayls painted Elizabeth Pepys "in the posture we saw one of my Lady Peters, like a St. Katherine"; a compliment to Queen Catherine and a fashionable pose. In the print at least, the features are heavy, and the whole picture is set solidly into an artificial, seventeenth century convention of fashionable low-cut dress, formal

84

curls, and the palm of martyrdom. The picture is static, rounded. Yet the whole portrait shows a young and beautiful lady who has about her, curiously, an innocence, a youth, a simplicity of nature, which the conformity in dress and pose to the fashion of the Court emphasizes.

Pepys gives only two details about her portrait: the background and the color of his wife's face. He watched the painting of the portrait "which," he wrote, "I like mighty well, and there had the pleasure to see how suddenly he draws the Heavens, laying a darke ground and then lightening it when and where he will." But as usual he gives no color. His wife's complexion had a glowing pallor Pepys thought lovely. Pepys put in the Diary after the first sitting: "But strange how like [to his wife's pallor] his very first dead colouring is, that it did me good to see it, and pleases me mightily." In Savill's portrait, too, "the dead colour of my wife is good, above all I expected, which pleased me extremely."

He paid Hayls 14 pounds for the picture and 25 shillings for the frame, and he thought the price "not a whit too deare for so good a picture. It is not yet quite finished and dry, so as to be fit to bring home yet. This day I begun to sit" (March 17, 1666).

Samuel Cooper was one of the great English miniaturists. He painted Elizabeth Pepys in the summer of 1668. He was fifty-nine then, and was held to be a man and a painter of the highest ability and culture, as he had been held by Cromwell and others of the Commonwealth whom he had painted. Six years before they met, (January 2, 1662), Pepys had called him "Cooper, the great limner in little," and after he had gone to Mr. Cooper's house and for the first time had seen his paintings (Mar. 30, 1668) he had been "infinitely satisfied." Cooper's paintings were "so extraordinary, as I do never expect to see the like again." Pepys seems somewhat subdued by Cooper's ability and his large social experience and his charm. He "do work finely . . . now I understand his great skill in musick, his playing and setting to the French lute most excellently; and [he] speaks French, and indeed is an excellent man" (July 10, 1668). Pepys's last entry, when he took his wife's miniature home, sums up his high opinion of Cooper and his independence in judging the portrait: "So away to Cooper's, where I spent all the afternoon with my wife and girl; seeing him make an end of her picture, which he did to my great content, though not so great as, I confess, I expected, being not satisfied in the greatness of the resemblance, nor in the blue garment: but it is most certainly a most rare piece of work, as to the painting. He hath £30 for his work [Savill had 3 pounds for his]—and the chrystal, and case, and gold case comes to £8. 3s. 4d; and which I sent him this night, that I might be out of debt" (August 10, 1668). This miniature cannot be traced.

The best portrait of Elizabeth Pepys is the white marble bust in St. Olave's Church, which, worn from 300 years of the climate and fortunes of London, seems to have the charm and vividness and beauty Pepys gave her in the Diary.

A Chronicle

William Penn the younger grew from fifteen to twenty-four (1660-1669) in the years the Diary was being kept and among the many people it tells of. All those years his home was the house where it was being written. There his father and sister and, after 1664, his mother and young brother lived. The happenings in Penn's family which Pepys records may be monotonous to a reader and may seem unimportant, but they filled much of Penn's boyhood and later, and they deserve the emphasis of repetition which the Diary gives. However prejudiced and thin and unperceiving and broken Pepys's entries about Penn may be, for much of Penn's character and qualities and occupations he did not care for and does not suggest or see, they give one view of him from the time he was fifteen years old until he was almost twenty-five.

Pepys's entries tell great events—war, plague, fire, death, changes in government and religion, the ending of the Commonwealth, the King and his Court. They tell, too, usual day-by-day matters of clothing and food, customs and ways of talk and the substance of household talk, books, pleasures, and serious occupations. And outside the direct mentions of Penn, in entries which seem not to touch him at all, Pepys shows the form and spirit of the Restoration, the colors and tones and shadings, the opinions and actions and ethics of seventeenth century society. He shows the questions and conditions which pressed in upon the times, and which Penn would have to accept or reject—or stay indifferent to; or, uneasily conscious of fault, leave untouched; or, as only a few did, find his new answers.

The whole Diary, then, adds some understanding and some facts about the persons and surroundings which affected—perhaps strongly perhaps not—Penn's faith and action; for the Diary registers temperatures and winds and sunshine and air-pressure and storms of the sixteen-sixties.

Sir William Penn (1621-1670)

Penn's father, Admiral Sir William Penn, was in 1660 a distinguished and able officer, knighted at the Restoration, an M. P., thirty-nine years old (twelve years older than Pepys), and one of the three Commissioners of the Navy. He lived next to Pepys at the Navy Office. In business and neighbourly closeness, Pepys saw him every day. The Diary names him more than 630 times. Yet after the easy months of first acquaintance, Pepys settled to the lasting opinion, strongest under exasperation, that Sir William was "an impertinent coxcomb" (1662), and (1665) "as false a man as ever lived," this last, on finding out what he thought a special trickery. Pepys went even to an Iago-like extreme of "who I hate with all my heart for his base treacherous tricks, but yet I think it not policy to declare it yet" (July 5, 1662). Pepys, as a child might, often dramatised the feeling he had: he over-stated it, simplified and intensified it, posed it and foreshortened it. But unlike a child he did not quickly forget. Pepys always was sure Sir William never deserved his trust, much less his friendship.

All the while, he and Sir William went on in what seemed friendly intimacy at the office and at home. They worked together at the Admiralty. When Sir William was in Ireland or for a day or so was out of London, Pepys watched his house and his affairs; and while Pepys was in the whirlpool of making over his house or was away from town, Sir William helped him with lodging or care. And the families dined together, traded opinions serious and light, sat together at St. Olave's, played cards and ate and walked and went visiting together, and such times were usually, as Pepys wrote, "very merry." Pepys and Sir William even were partners in timber-buying and sea-business when the Diary ends.

Some entries Pepys made in the second year of his clerkship suggest why he felt as he did about Sir William.

The Surveyor of the Navy in 1660 was Sir William Batten. He was about sixty-three or sixty-four; an admiral; an M. P.; a rough, stocky ("thick to [his] length"), coarse, successful, hard-living sea-officer; he was the old commander under whom, Sir William told Pepys one morning, he had been "bred up" as a seaman (August 21, 1660). Sir William Batten had been an officer in the Admiralty of Charles I, and had grown wealthy enough to have an estate in Essex, but he and his family lived most of the time in the Navy Office. Pepys was likeable. When he first became Clerk, Batten and Penn took him up for a companion at the office and in evenings at taverns. Pepys did not care much for their company, day or evening, but the tavern evenings pleased him well enough, even if they cost him more than he could afford and left him uncertain in body the next morning.

The first week of December, when Pepys had been Clerk for a year and a half, the three went on Navy business to Whitehall. After they had signed there in the afternoon a contract between the government and the East India Company and were ready to drive home, "Sir W. Batten offer[ed] to go to the 3 Tuns at Charing Cross, where the pretty maid the daughter of the house is." Pepys turned the offer into some joke, which as he worded it, "tickled" Penn (angered and irritated him). Pepys saw that the joke had gone wrong and he abruptly took leave to speak with a Court officer. They waited for him, which pleased Pepys, and all of them drove home together in Sir William Penn's coach, "but no words passed between him and me in all our way home" (December 6, 1661). Yet the next day he and Penn were working together, and the afternoon of the eleventh—"very cold"—Pepys and Sir William, who for a few days had not been well, walked an hour or two in Moorfields, as they had before. The same day Elizabeth Pepys drove to Clerkenwell to see Peg Penn, at school there. Sir William Batten was out of town.

December 21, two weeks after his inopportune joke, Pepys was late at a committee meeting with Batten and Penn. One of them said, "without their Register they were not a Committee." Pepys resented that. He "took [it] in some dudgeon," for he was sure it was a reprimand, a pay-off for his joke over the Three Tuns. He was certain he was more than a keeper of their minutes. Pepys had a high opinion of himself and his office, and he was determined that others more established and older should value him fairly. He would not accept inferiority. He would fight whoever implied it. "I . . . see clearly that I must keep myself at a little distance with them and not crouch, or else I shall never keep myself up even with them." *Crouch* is the word. They must treat him with deserved respect. The Sir Williams were not to put him in his place—unless he himself defined it. So, all the next fortnight he did not see Sir William Batten, the more important of the two, having "resolved to keep myself more reserved to avoyd the contempt which otherwise I must fall into." He did go to Sir William Batten's the fifth, at the end of the fortnight. After the first visit, he was often there, and seems to have found no attempt at superiority in Sir William. He went Wednesday that week and again Saturday, and he enjoyed the talk at Sir William's, especially about the curious customs in the election of the Dukes of Genoa. Eight months later (August 6) Sir William, "much troubled," told Pepys as they walked in the garden "he did see there was a design of bringing another man in his room" and had taken notice of Pepys's sorting himself against him. Pepys assured Sir William he was not against him. He judged that "he perceives himself tottering." To Pepys, he seemed "going down the wind in every body's esteem." That appeal reversed the position of Sir William Batten and Pepys.

With Sir William Penn, Pepys went on easily at the Office and outside it. They walked and dined and supped and "sat and talked and drank together" quite as usual; around Christmas, more than usual, for William Penn, the son, was home from Oxford and Peg from her school in North London. Through the holidays Penn and his children and Pepys and Elizabeth Pepys were together constantly and pleasantly. No outside sounds from the tension of December 6 and December 21 seem to have come into the quiet.

William Penn (1644-1718)

William Penn, Sir William's oldest child, Pepys names in the Diary 25 times. They are off-hand, brief comments, from casual interest. They begin when William Penn was sixteen and end when he was about twenty-four. They have the value of being the impressions of a shrewd if prejudiced man, not much interested in young Penn, who for a while, saw him often and heard his family and others talk to him, and who was free from the bias of knowing that Will Pen became William Penn of Pennsylvania. And Pepys, when as in most of the Diary he was not thinking of William Penn, makes real the world which Penn grew up in and which helped educate him.

William Penn comes into the Diary first, April 22, 1661. Pepys and "Sir W. Pen and his son" with others, watched the King, after the ancient custom, enter the City the morning before he was crowned. Through all splendid procession, "Embroidery and diamonds were ordinary . . ." and, in the bright sun "So glorious was the show with gold and silver, that . . . our eyes at last [were] overcome with it." William Penn that day counts for only two words, "his son." He was sixteen and a half years old, up from Oxford, where he had matriculated at Christ Church six months earlier, in October, 1660. Until a little before that time he was with his mother in Ireland, for three years, being tutored.

Pepys next wrote of him the first of November, 1661. That eve-

89

ning Sir William, and "his son, Mr. William Pen, lately come from Oxford," supped at Pepys's house and "were very merry till late." Lady Penn and young Richard were not in London until three years later, when on August 19, 1664, Pepys and Elizabeth Pepys went "to Sir William Pen's to see his lady the first time." She had been in Ireland, looking after their estate.

Through Christmas and New Year's Sir William and the two children and Pepys and Elizabeth Pepys often dined and supped together and followed holiday customs. The Diary gives their occupations and interests, and the people among whom they lived, and so makes clear details of Will Penn's daily life even when he is not spoken of.

Christmas Day, 1661, after hearing "A good sermon" at St. Olave's, Pepys and his wife had dinner at home, alone. At dinner he took "occasion from some fault in the meat to complain of [the] maid's sluttery," and they fell out and he "went up to [his] chamber in a discontent." Soon his wife came to him and in their, happily, usual way "all friends again." The day was sunny and so they "did walk upon the leads." Then "Sir W. Pen called us, and we went to his house and supped with him." Before supper "Captain Cock came to us half drunk," and talkative. Sir William, "knowing his humour and that there was no end of his talking, drinks [with him] four great glasses of wine . . . one after another, healthe to the king," in which the captain could not refuse to join, "and by that means made him drunk, and so he went away," speechless. Then they "sat down to supper, and were merry." William Penn and his sister, it seems, were with them.

After dinner the next day, Sir William and his son and daughter and Pepys and Elizabeth Pepys went in Sir William's "coach to Moorfields to walk." Moorfields was just outside the City, to the north. It was open land, less formal than a park, with roads and walks, and taverns, and spaces for wrestlings and fairs and Punch and Judy shows, and for the assembling of Londoners. The day Pepys was at Moorfields was "most foul weather, and so we went into an alehouse and there eat some cakes and ale, and a washeall-bowle woman and girl came to us and sung to us." In the evening, at home, "Sir W. Pen and his son and daughter to supper to me to a good turkey, and were merry at cards." Friday, the twenty-seventh, was busy for Pepys. In the morning he ordered (did "bespeak") from his bookseller *Stephen's Thesaurus Graecae Linguae*, four volumes at 4 pounds, to give as prize books to his old school (The books never came, and a year later he bought the set at another

90

shop for 4 pounds and 10 shillings); heard a good sermon at St. Paul's Church; after dinner talked and drank wine with a man from the Exchequer and Mr. Knightly, a merchant ("better wine I never drank in all my life"); sent the Exchequer man, overcome, home to Westminster in a coach. Then, "finding my wife gone to Sir W. Pen's, I went thither and there, I sat and played at cards and supped."

Saturday, December 28, "in the afternoon all of us [were] at the office . . . making up of a speedy estimate of all the debts of the Navy, which is put into good forwardness" [is needed at once]. When he came home, Sir William was at the house, "who with his children staid playing cards late."

Sunday, Pepys had dinner at home, "chiefly to put off dining with Sir W. Pen to-day because Holmes dined there." Then he took his wife by coach to Westminster to see a friend they had made when they were first married, Mrs. Hunt. He went on to the Abbey. He met there the choirmaster, who "took me in among the quire, and there I sang with them their service." He and his wife went to the Wardrobe, Lady Sandwich's house, and supped and stayed very long, talking "with my Lady, who seems to dote every day more and more upon us." Major, later Sir Robert, Holmes, whom he avoided, was an old comrade of Sir William's, then thirty-eight, able but ill-mannered and impudent. Pepys thought him free toward Mrs. Pepys. He seems to have been generally disliked; Andrew Marvell, the poet, calls him a tough Irish boy and a "highway man"; the Admiralty reprimanded him for insolence; and he was sent to the Tower for not obeying Naval orders. Yet in 1665 he captured New Amsterdam from the Dutch. Four months before Pepys met him at Christmas, he had brought in his ship from Guinea, to Pepys's wonder, "a great baboon, like a man in most things . . . a monster. . . . I do believe that it already understands much English." They all were "called to Sir W. Batten's to see the strange creature," William Penn, it seems, included (August 24, 1661). William Penn encountered a variety of people in his father's house.

Monday, the thirtieth, Pepys worked again at the Naval estimate. Afterward he and Elizabeth Pepys and Sir William went to see the portraits Savill was painting of Pepys and his wife. Then, at the Mitre, he gave a dinner ("a great chine of beef, . . . with three barrels of oysters and three pullets, and plenty of wine and mirth") to all his old acquaintances of the Exchequer, about a dozen of them, and foolishly he promised such a dinner to them "this day twelvemonth, and so for ever while I live, but I do not intend it." When he came home, rather late, he found "Sir W. Pen, who with his children and my wife had been to a play to-day and saw [Chapman's Bussy] D'Ambois, which I never saw. Here we stayed late at supper and played at cards."

The next morning Pepys went with his wife for her last sitting ("her picture I think will please me very well.") It did. In the afternoon he worked, finishing the estimate of the Navy debts up to that day; they came to nearly £374,000. "So . . . after supper, and my barber had trimmed me, I sat down to end my journell for this year." He wrote a long summary, perhaps 400 words. The end of the next year, he wrote 2,600 words. He did not go to Sir William's that day.

The morning of New Year's, 1662, William Penn came and they walked out to the stationer's, where they "looked over some pictures and maps" for his house, and Pepys asked "young Mr. Pen and his sister to go anon with my wife and I to the Theatre." In the afternoon, at half-past two, "after [they] had eat a barrel of oysters," they went to *The Spanish Curate*, "well acted, and a good play," but not much of a story, of "no great content," and some parts "over-done." The young Penns "sat with us till late at night at cards very merry, but the jest was Mr. Pen had left his sword in the coach." Pepys's boy got it for him again. William Penn was eighteen.

January 2, 1662, Pepys worked all the morning, dined at Lady Sandwich's—"a good and great dinner" and noble company— and after working at his office till night and finishing other business he went home, and there "sat at my lute and singing till almost twelve at night." On the third he did much "petty businesses," dined at "my Lord Crew's [Lady Sandwich's father's] with him and his Lady," bought some engravings which were expensive, thought over his brother Tom's affairs and getting a wife for him, and in the evening at home was "much troubled . . . because of my present great expense," so troubled that he was "loth . . . to cast up and see how my estate stands."

"4th. At home most of the morning hanging up pictures, and seeing how my pewter sconces that I have bought will become my stayres and entry." Next he took his wife by boat to her father's in Westminster; heard a good dog story; dined with his wife at the Crown in King Street on roast beef and a mutton pie and a mince pie, "but none of them pleased me." He and his wife went home, and he worked until late at his office, and at length they "to Sir W. Pen's to cards and supper." That day he wrote that he realized "much correspondence there has been between our two families all this Christmas." Even when they were not together, their patterns of daily occupation ran on much alike.

The fifth was Sunday. His wife was unwell and he went alone to church and "dined alone upon some marrow bones, and had a fine piece of rost beef, but being alone I eat nothing": typical of Pepys. After dinner he talked with his brother Tom about Tom's possible marriage; went again to church, where he gave the sexton three shillings "for this last year" and was much amused when the Clerk by mistake tried to sing the words of one song to the tune of another. He went after church, the first time in two weeks, to Sir W. Batten's. Those were the two weeks just after the committee episode and his determination not to cringe. In the evening he stayed at "home and sat and talked and supped" with his wife, and at length went to bed after prayers and the writing of a letter on the important, long drawn-out "business of striking of flags"— the need for a foreign ship to lower its flag to the flag of an English warship in British waters.

The chronicle of intimacy runs on. The sixth of January, Twelfth Night, was a solemn feast day which Sir William held on the anniversary of his wedding. Pepys and Elizabeth Pepys with others dined at Sir William's, "and we had, besides a good chine of beef and other good cheer, eighteen mince pies in a dish, the number of the years that he hath been married." Lady Penn was still in Ireland. Pepys did not enjoy the dinner. Major Holmes again tried to be free with Mrs. Pepys, who disliked his attempts. After dinner "they set in to drinking, so that I would stay no longer, but went away home." Rather incomprehensibly, Captain Cock, quite drunk, followed them, sat awhile, bewildered, and "so away." Late in the afternoon, Pepys went back to Sir William's, where, the others having gone, he "sat and played at cards with Sir W. Pen and his children," had supper, and went home. Even at home he found the discomfort of his day not ended. Will Hewer had, he thought, drunk too much. Pepys threatened to dismiss him. At last he went up to bed and told his wife all that had happened. That done, he slept.

The next morning, he lay "Long in bed, and then rose and went along with Sir W. Pen on foot to Stepny to Mrs. Chappell's (who has the pretty boy to her son)." He met his wife and Sir William and the children at Mrs. Chappell's, and they dined there and were happy, and he went by coach home to his office. In the afternoon he and his wife went to "Sir W. Pen's, . . . supped and played at cards . . . and were merry, the children being to go all away to school again tomorrow"—William to Oxford and Peg to her finishing school at Clerkenwell.

In the Diary the next two weeks are blank of William Penn. Then, on Saturday, January 25, "Walking in the garden to give the gardener directions what to do this year (for I intend to have the garden handsome), Sir W. Pen came to me, and did break a business to me about removing his son from Oxford to Cambridge." Pepys proposed Magdalene, his own college, and promised "to write about it." He did not know why the change was to be made. Seven weeks later, he and Sir William (Sunday, March 16) again spent an hour in the garden. That night his wife and he had supper at Sir William's: "his son William is at home not well. But all things, I fear do not go well with them; they look discontentedly, but I know not what ails them." Lady Penn still was in Ireland. William Penn, Pepys found five weeks later, had been expelled from Oxford about March 1. Monday, April 28, Pepys jotted: "Sir W. Pen much troubled upon letters came last night. Showed me one of Dr. Owen's to his son, whereby it appears his son is much perverted in his opinion by him; which I now perceive is one thing that hath put Sir William so long off the hooks." William Penn had been at home eight weeks. Dr. Owen was a non-conformist minister, appointed dean of Christ Church, William Penn's college, by Cromwell in 1653, and "ejected" in 1660. Penn and "other students, withdrawing from the National Way of Worship . . . preached and prayed among themselves." And Penn refused to attend chapel.

After April, Pepys did not write of Penn for almost two months and a half. Then, on July 5, he had Sir William (still up to "his base treacherous tricks") and his son to dinner. "I having some venison given me a day or two ago . . . had a shoulder roasted, another baked, and the umbles [liver, heart, and such] baked in a pie, and all very well done. We were merry . . . and the more because I would not seem otherwise to Sir W. Pen, he being within a day or two to go for Ireland." Before he went, he came on the ninth to Pepys's office, "to take his leave . . . and desiring a turn in the garden, did commit the care of his building to me, and offered all his services to me in all matters of mine." (The roofs on their houses and Sir William Batten's were to be raised and other changes made). "I did, God forgive me! promise him all my service and love."

94

After that, William Penn drops from the Diary for two years. To William Penn the five months from early spring to mid-summer in 1662—March through July—was a changing, deeply troubled time. He had been sent down from Oxford; had been at home "not well" (as Pepys knew); had been more and more at odds with his father about Oxford and his future (as Pepys guessed); had been argued with, commanded, beaten, put out of the house with no money, and disinherited, for his father expected obedience as part of affection. Penn himself, fifteen years later, told a congregation in Holland that after he was expelled ("banisht the College" he called it and left the cause of it clouded, though not his opinion of Oxford) "bitter Usage I underwent when I returned to my Father; whipping, beating and turning out of doors in 1662." (*Travails in Holland and Germany*, London, 1694, First Edition, Darlington Library, p. 182). He was taken back by his father, and the last of July he was sent on the Grand Tour.

Penn's first biographer, supposed to be Joseph Besse, writing eight years after his death, says much the same. He writes: Penn "not at all abating the Fervour of his *Zeal*, he was at length, for persevering in the like Religious Practices, expell'd the *College*.

"From thence he returned Home, but still took great *Delight* in the Company of ... *Religious People,* which his Father ... endeavoured both by Words and Blows to deter him from; but finding those Methods ineffectual, he was at length so incensed, that he turn'd him out of Doors." Later "his Father's Affection ... subdu'd his *Anger,* who then sent him to *France,* in Company with some *Persons of Quality,* that were making a Tour thither." (*A Collection of the Works of William Penn,* 2 vols., folio, London, 1726, attributed to Joseph Besse.)

The Grand Tour on which he set out in July with money, aristocratic company, and the right letters of introduction, was to finish his education, form his character, and refine his manners and taste. He spent the first four months in Paris, still among "persons of rank and quality" at the court of Louis XIV, the school to all Europe, and then for almost a year and a half he studied, as many young Englishmen did during the Commonwealth and the Monarchy, at the Protestant college in Saumur, an ancient town in western France, on the Loire. In January 1664 he started again his leisurely travels through France and Switzerland, and he was in northern Italy, at Turin, late in the summer, when a letter from his father called him home. England had declared war on Holland and was uneasy in the shadow of the Plague spreading north through Europe. The last week in August he was home. Lady Penn and her son Dicke had come from Ireland ten days earlier.

The next two months, time stood still for him. It went by without his accepting responsibility or taking a career. To those about him it was a serious time, and they kept hard at work. Pepys and Sir William were all the summer in London strengthening the Navy, for the Dutch "crewsed up and down the Channel with 22 ships of warr," to defend their fishing fleet they had written King Charles: he had laughed. The Plague, brought from Algiers, had increased greatly in Amsterdam during May, and was reported to have killed fifty sailors in Cadiz in June. Its coming to England seemed sure. Yet through the early fall Penn was quite at leisure, a young gentleman just home from foreign courts and travel.

His first biographer wrote that "upon his Return, his Father [found] him not only a good Proficient in the *French Tongue,* but also perfectly accomplished with a *Polite* and *Courtly Behaviour* . . . and indeed for some Time after his Return from *France,* his Carriage was such as justly entitled him to the Character of a *Compleat Young Gentleman.*" Yet "Great, about this Time, was his *Spiritual Conflict; His Blooming Youth.* His *Natural Inclination,* His *Lively* and *Active Disposition,* His *Acquired Accomplishments* [were at war with] the earnest Supplication of his Soul" *(A Collection* etc., vol. I, p. 2). Pepys and Elizabeth Pepys, of course, knew nothing of this conflict.

In the next two months Penn was often with Pepys. At the end of his entry for Friday, August 26, 1664, Pepys wrote: "This day my wife tells me Mr. Pen, Sir William's son, is come back from France, and come to visit her. A most modish person, grown, she says a fine gentleman." Pepys then was thirty-one, his wife was twenty-four, Sir William was forty-three, Lady Penn was about forty-six, William Penn was almost twenty, and Peg and young Richard about twelve and eight.

William Penn, who had called first on Friday, called again on Tuesday. "[A]fter dinner comes Mr. Penn to visit me, and staid an houre talking with me. I perceive something of learning he hath got, but a great deal, if not too much, of the vanity of the French garbe and affected manner of speech and gait. I fear all real profit he hath made of his travel will signify little" (August 30, 1664). This was the first impression Pepys had after the absence for two years on the Grand Tour.

William Penn called the next Monday. When Pepys came home in the afternoon, he "was troubled to find [his] wife . . . expecting

Mr. Penn," who had already come three times that day and had been "by her people [servants] denied, which . . . she thought not fit he should be any more. But yet even this did raise my jealousy . . . and much vex me." William Penn, however, did not come that day; "which pleased me" (September 5, 1644). Elizabeth Pepys was four years older than Penn.

Again, September 14, when Pepys came home, he found "Mr. Pen come to visit my wife." Penn was still with them when Pepys was "sent for" by Mr. Bland, a wealthy merchant going to Tangiers three weeks later, with whom Pepys had an appointment for supper. Against his will, Pepys "left them together, but, God knows without any reason of fear . . . of any evil between them, but such is my natural folly." Mr. Bland and his wife, however, "very civilly went forth and brought her and W. Pen . . . and we supped nobly."

Then a change came. Pepys did not write of Penn until four months and a half later, when at the end of January 29 he met him by chance. The entry only touches Penn. Except as a name he is not in it. Of the evening, Pepys gives a lively account, which shows a fairly constant part of Penn's life in London. Pepys went late, after supper, to Sir William Batten's. Sir William seemed more short and stout and rough than ever. The occasion emphasized him. With him were Sir William Penn, William Penn, the Lieutenant of the Tower, and two most successful City merchants, one in woolens and one in leather. Batten, the Lieutenant, and the City merchants had, it appeared, supped well. Pepys listened to "a great deal of sorry disordered talk. . . . Lord! to see how void of method and sense their discourse was, and in what heat, insomuch that Sir R. Ford [the wool merchant, Sheriff of London, member of Tangier Commission] (who we judged, some of us, to be a littled foxed) fell into very high terms with Sir W. Batten" and others. Pepys knew Sir Richard was "a very able man of his brains and his tongue, and a scholler," and not at all what Pepys called a "bufflehead." So, Pepys says, "I see that no man is wise at all times."

From the Sunday evening in January until the end of the Diary, Pepys wrote only four times of meeting Penn: once in April, before his father's sea victory in June and the start of the Plague in London, and three times in September after the victory, at the height of the Plague.

April 25, a critical time, six months after Sir William had gone to the "Royal Charles" and six weeks before the battle, Pepys made the entry: "This afternoon W. Pen, lately come from his father in the fleete, did give me an account how the fleete did sayle, about 103 in all, besides small catches, they being in sight of six or seven Dutch scouts, and sent ships in chase of them."

When the summer was over and the war—though not the Plague—had lessened, there came in September the last meetings told of in the Diary. The first week in September, when Pepys went home Tuesday the fifth, he found there, after the old habit, "W. Pen, and he staid supper with us and mighty merry talking of his travels and the French humours, etc., and so parted." A week later, by chance at Greenwich, Pepys "saw Mr. Pen walking my way (September 13, 1665), and so we walked together," and, perhaps maliciously, Pepys "for discourse . . . put him into talk of France." William Penn "took delight to tell me of his observations, some good, some impertinent, and all ill told, yet it served for want of better." Pepys and his wife later that day supped at the Penn's, and "After supper Mr. Pen and I fell to discourse about some words in a French song my wife was saying" [singing]. William Penn set Pepys right about the meaning. Pepys backed his own translation 20 to 1. They counter-talked of the phrase for "an houre and more upon the dispute," got "almost angry," and "at last broke up not satisfied" when Pepys went home. "I knew myself in the right." Penn was never drawn to Pepys or open with him. He showed to Pepys the surface Pepys expected.

There were causes for their not meeting often in London. Pepys at the Navy Office was working hard to strengthen the fleet with ships and men and supplies, a necessary and unending and difficult business, Parliament being as it was and the Dutch pressing the weight of the war. Penn, after his interlude of leisure, had his own serious matters for two years. Besides, he did not much care to be with Pepys.

A summary of the two years for him (from early November 1664 to early January 1666) runs: two months after he came from the Grand Tour, his father was appointed (November 7, 1664) Great Captain Commander of the Duke of York's flagship "Royal Charles," and so, in effect, was second in command on the Channel Fleet; he enrolled at Lincoln's Inn on February 7, 1665; while he was at Lincoln's Inn he often went to his father and at times carried dispatches from the Duke and his father to the King; on June 3 his father won the great battle off Lowestoft; in early June the Plague broke out in the City, close to Seething Lane; and then, at the end of the two years, Sir William being home, Penn being twenty-two and his law study over, the intensity of the Dutch War having let up for a time and the Plague fading, he went to Ireland. He went there chiefly to use his law on the tangle of the Irish estate. His mother and sister and young brother, and, at the last, his father were in London.

In the two years before he went to Ireland, the years he was twenty and twenty-one, three matters filled a good part of Penn's life—his study at Lincoln's Inn, being with his father on the "Royal Charles," and the Plague close around him.

After he had enrolled at Lincoln's Inn in February, he found the law took much of his time and filled much of his interest. As the great Lord Chief Justice Coke had said of the law, "the same is an act which requires long study and experience before that a man can attain to the cognizance of it." Penn did not give the law all Coke defined for it, but he did study it, and later used it and found it served him well through many years in England and America. Lincoln's Inn was a foundation with a noble history, and it was beautifully housed, a place for learning and a school for the sons of gentlemen. Penn was registered there as *William Penn, son and heir apparent of Sir William Penn, of City of London, Knight.* Law was the center and the constant of their studies, but Shakespeare, and Beaumont and Fletcher, and other poets were read. Jonson was remembered. The young men gave plays and masques and revels, to one of which Pepys saw the King going in state with his life-guards. Evelyn, who was at another of the revels, wrote that it began with a "grand masque"—music and a play and dances— and that its actors, the students, were "gloriously clad," and that it ended "in a magnificent banquet." Lincoln's Inn was almost two miles from Seething Lane, across London to the west, outside the walls.

In London, during the Plague, Penn lived for two years in the midst of pestilence and great distress, as he tells in his *Travails,* and he came to know closely ways of life he had not known before and people he had never before been close to. The differences in what Pepys and William Penn were doing, and their difference in character and temper and interest and aims and even in age, separated them in 1665 and after, though they lived for years in the same house and to both of them the Plague and the war were intimate. Pepys was even interested in the law. He bought four or five volumes of Lord Chief Justice Coke's and thought them "very fine noble readings" (1665) and "mighty well worth reading, and do inform me in many things" (1667).

99

June 3, 1665, the English fleet won a great victory. For eight months, after early November, it had been on guard in the Channel. By late May, London was expecting an immediate battle. Then, June 8, Pepys put in capitals across his page: *"VICTORY OVER THE DUTCH, JUNE 3RD, 1665."* The Dutch in the battle off Lowestoft lost their admiral Van Tromp and "about 24 of their best ships; [had] killed and taken near 8 or 10,000 men and [we] lost, we think not above 700.... They are all fled ... and we in pursuit.... A great [er] victory never known in the world." Pepys admits that Sir William in command of the Duke's flagship did "good service indeed." As soon as Pepys heard "the great news newly at last come," he went with his "heart full of joy, home [where Elizabeth Pepys was], and to my office a little; then to my Lady Pen's, where they are all [Pepys does not say William Penn was one but it seems probable he was] joyed and not a little puffed up at the good success of their father." They had a "great bonefire at the gate and walked out down into the streete." Pepys gave the boys four shillings, and then he went home and to bed, his "heart at great rest and quiett, saving that the consideration of the victory is too great for me ... to comprehend."

Sir William's part in the battle was one cause of the King's granting William Penn his charter for Pennsylvania in 1680. In the charter the King praises "the memory and merits of Sir William Penn in divers services, and particularly his conduct, courage, and discretion under our dearest brother, James, Duke of York, in that signal battle and victory fought and obtained against the Dutch fleet ... in 1665." Possibly, Pepys was ungenerous in his praise of Sir William.

* * * * * *

What Pepys wrote about Penn in 1665 and Penn's letters to his father that summer are a strange contrast. Pepys wrote of him as "merry," light-minded, fairly intelligent, elegant, immature, young. Penn, who two days before he saw Pepys had come to London with dispatches to the King from his father and the Duke of York, wrote: "Honoured Father ... I pray God, after all the foul weather and dangers you are exposed to ... that you come home ... secure. And, I bless God, my heart does not in any way fail; but firmly believes, that if God has called you out to battle, he will cover your head in that smoky day ... your concerns are most dear to me."

The first week of May he was again carrying dispatches to the King. Pepys does not say he saw him. Penn wrote to his father on the sixth that he landed at Harwich "about one of the clock" on Sunday, posted at three o'clock to London, "and was in London the next morning by almost daylight." He "hasted to Whitehall." The King was not up, but "he was informed there was an express from the duke: at which, earnestly skipping out of his bed, he came only in his gown and slippers; who, when he saw me, said, 'Oh! is't you? how is Sir William?' He asked how you did at three several times. . . . After interrogating me above half an hour, he bid me go now about your business, and mine too." The ending of this letter seems unusual, for it is not at all the conventional phrasing of a dutiful, twenty-one-year-old, seventeenth-century son, and is wholly different from the "mighty merry talking" and much else Pepys told of Penn. He ended his letter: "I pray God be with you, and be your armour in the day of controversy! May that power be your salvation, for his name's sake! and so will he wish and pray, that is, with all true veneration,/ Honoured father,/ Your obedient son and servant,/ William Penn." Penn soon was back with the fleet. To Pepys and to Sir William, Penn at twenty-one spoke with infinite difference.

In the early spring of 1666 Penn crossed to Ireland to use his law on his father's Irish estate. He was in Ireland a year and a half. At first he was at the court of the viceroy, an old friend of his father's. There he volunteered against Irish rebels, served well in the campaign, was offered a permanent command, and for a while was sure he wanted to be a soldier. His portrait in armor was painted about that time. Sir William vetoed the army and set Penn to work again on the tangles of the estate. Penn got to work on them. In Cork, one day late in the summer or early fall of 1667, he went to a meeting of Quakers, and there he heard Thomas Loe preach on the faith that overcomes the world. Thomas Loe was a middle-aged tradesman and Quaker preacher. Once when Penn was thirteen Loe had "much impressed" him by his talk with Sir William at Sir William's house in Ireland. It was to hear Loe again that Penn, finding by chance he was to preach, had gone to the meeting.

To set the exact dates of what happened in Cork when Penn was becoming a Quaker seems impossible. Penn himself in 1677 said only that during the Plague the Lord had given him "a deep sense . . . of the Vanity of this World," and that in the Plague time he uttered "Mournful and Bitter Cries to him that he should be shown his own way of Life and Salvation," and that "after all this the glory of the world over-took me [seemingly, in part, while he

101

was in Ireland] and I was even ready to give up myself unto, it!" *(Travails,* Frst Edition, p. 182). Penn goes on, "it was at this time that the Lord visited me with a certain sound and testimony of his eternal Word, through one of those the World calls a *Quaker.*" The place, certainly, was Cork. The Quaker was Thomas Loe. The time is not given exactly.

Penn kept going to the meetings. At one, September 3, (exact in the record), he put out of the meeting a soldier bent on disturbance. Whether or not he had earlier become a Quaker is not clear. Sir William in London hearing the news from Cork wrote a short and definite letter to his son from the Navy Office, October 12, 1667: "Sonne William I have writt several ters to yo since I recd any fr you. By this I agayne charge yo & strictly comand that yo come to mee with all possible speeds in expectation of yo complyance. I remayne yo aff father W. Penn." Ten days later he wrote again, "... to charge yo to repair to mee with all posable speede ... & not to make any stay ... any place ... untill it please God you see me. Yr very afft father." Upon this definite but not harsh command, Penn travelled home, slowly, knowing his father's plan for him and his father's strength and affection, dreading conflict, and praying he might stand firm against opposition. His meeting with his father was violent and intensely unhappy for each. Penn did not give way. Then and later, Penn said in 1677, there "fell upon me, the Displeasure of my Parents, ... the strangeness of all my Companions, what a Sign and Wonder they made of me; but, above all, that great Cross of resisting and watching against my own Inward vain Affections and Thoughts."

What day Penn came to London is not told. The closest to exactness is Pepys's entry, December 29, 1667, "that Mr. William Pen, ... is lately come over from Ireland."

An explanation here may help to make clearer both Pepys's later entries and Penn's conversion. Religious mysticism, "mystical pietism" the *Dictionary of National Biography* calls it, had always been strong in William Penn and his education may have strengthened it. He first went to school when he was five or six, at Chigwell, a "stronghold of Puritanism" (DNB). In his *Travails* (published 1694), he writes that the Lord first appeared to him when he was about twelve and that in the next three years "the Lord visited me, and [gave] divine impressions ... of himself." He tells of his "Persecution at *Oxford;* how the Lord sustained me in the midst of that hellish darkness and debauchery"; of "bitter Usage" at home, in 1662; of "the Lord's dealings with me in *France,* and in the time of the great Plague in *London*"; of "the deep sense he gave me of the Vanity of this World" and of "my Mournful and Bitter Cries to him that he would show me his own way of Life and Salvation." All this he had experienced before he went to Ireland in 1666. And all this was unknown to Pepys.

After William Penn went to Ireland in January, 1666, Pepys did not say he ever saw him. He did, however, write of him in the Diary four times more. Two of these give "news"—gossip—Mrs. Turner told him. Mrs. Turner was the wife of Thomas Turner, a minor official in the Navy Office. Twenty years before, when Turner was a petty naval officer, they had been intimates of Sir William's. Mrs. Turner was a middle-aged, talkative, disappointed woman, inquisitive about happenings in the Navy Building, where she, too, lived. In 1644 she had been a close (and persistent) neighbor of the Penns, when, newly married, they lived in Great Tower Street, in two rooms "one over another." There William Penn was born. Turner had been his godparent; she, Peg's, in 1652.

Twenty years later, she held a strong grudge against Sir William and Lady Penn, mainly for benefits forgot and for Sir William's success. Her gossip was constant and coloured and malicious. Endlessly, she picked up trifles to the discredit of the Penns. Pepys listened to her.

The afternoon of May 21, 1667, though "it went against my heart to go away from the very door of the Duke's playhouse, and my Lady Castlemayne's coach." (The Duke's Company was playing *The Siege of Rhodes*), Pepys walked on to his office, cleared up much work, and toward evening went home to his wife, who was ill with a cold: "much better than going to a play." He sat with her and read aloud to her from *The Grand Cyrus*, in English. That is one side of Pepys—and very likeable. In the evening, Mrs. Turner came to sit and talk with them. After a little, Elizabeth Pepys went to bed. Pepys and Mrs. Turner sat "up till 12 at night talking alone in my chamber, and most of our discourse was of our neighbors"; kitchen gossip, from servants, third-hand. She told him the "very poor and mean" and extravagent ways of Lord Bruncker and Mrs. Williams, who lived with him, though he hath "another . . . he keeps in Convent Garden." They owed everyone, "even Mrs. Shipman for her butter and cheese about £3." Then Mrs. Turner "fell to talk of Sir W. Pen, and his family and rise," and their low condition and poverty in 1644, Sir William "was a pityfull fellow," Mrs. Turner said; "his rise hath been [by] his giving of large bribes"; he turned "Roundhead . . . when he . . . saw fit"; he "was

in the late war a devilish plunderer, and that got him his estate
... in Ireland and nothing else." Lady Penn, when Mrs. Turner
had first known her, "was one of the sourest, dirty women, that
ever she saw," a "dirty slattern, with her stockings hanging about
her heels" until Mrs. Turner made as much of a lady of her as was
possible. The "people of the whole Hill did say that Mrs. Turner
had made Mrs. Pen a gentlewoman." The four of them had been
as brothers and sisters. Sir William had risen "by her and her husband's means, and it is a most inconceivable thing how this man
can have the face to use her and her family with the neglect that
he do them." And "his son was a babbler and one like his father
and worse." Pepys set down Mrs. Turner's talk as all true, facts
and feeling. "Upon the whole, she told me stories enough to con-
firm me that he [Sir William] is the most false fellow that ever was
born of woman, and that so she thinks and knows him to be."

Sunday, four days after Christmas, "At night comes Mrs. Turner
to see us; and there, among other talk, she tells me that Mr. William Pen, who is lately come over from Ireland, is a Quaker again,
or some very melancholy thing; that he cares for no company, nor
comes into any: which is a pleasant thing, after his being abroad
so long, and his father such a hypocritical rogue, and at this time
an Atheist." The main point of Mrs. Turner's news was true: Penn
had become a Quaker.

Twice after that, Pepys wrote of Penn. The first entry, October
12, 1668, is "this night my bookseller Shrewsbury ... brings my
books ... and after supper to read a ridiculous nonsensical book
set out by Will Pen, for the Quakers; but so full of nothing but
nonsense, that I was ashamed to read in it." This pamphlet, *Truth
Exalted* (1668), was a short tract of about 4,600 words, written from
Newgate, where William Penn was imprisoned. His prison was so
"noisesome and stinking" a place that it was "an unfit sty for swine."
The title page of this tract gives fairly well its tone.

*TRUTH EXALTED: in A short, but sure, Testimony against all
those Religions, Faiths, and Worships that have been formed and
followed in the darkness of Apostacy—And for that Glorious Light
which is now risen, and shines forth in the Life and Doctrine of the
despised Quakers, as the alone good old way of Life and Salvation.
Presented to Princes, Priests, and People, that they may repent,
believe, and obey. BY William Penn the Younger, whom Divine
Love constrains in a holy contempt to trample on Egypt's glory,
not fearing the Kings wrath, having beheld the Magisty of him
who is Invisible. London, Printed in the Year, 1668.*

104

Truth Exalted is a full-voiced, youthful, thundering assault, sure of its unique authority and knowledge. "Calamity, Pining, and Distress . . . Terrible Destruction" waited, their hands strong and opened, to grasp the people of England unless they forsook "Father, Mother, Sister, Brother, House, Land, Husband or wife . . . with Silence and Fear to wait in this Glorious Light" displayed for the "contemned *Quakers* to walk in." All other beliefs—Catholic, Protestant, Non-conformists—were lures of the cloven-footed devil, "that Subtil Serpent." Anthems and altars and colored windows, bowing, candles and vestments, rituals, the great churches, liturgies and responses, organs and choirs and other music, pictures, set forms of prayer, founts, all outward forms and symbols were "dirty Trash," "wholly evil," deceits of hell, feeding the fire which burned for men inexstinguishably. Schools and universities were evil, "Signal places for Idleness, Looseness, Prophaneness, Prodigality, and gross Ignorance," places of "hellish darkness and debauchery." The culture and forms of society, too, were evil, and the vain scribblings called books. "O tremble and Quake . . . O ye Idolatrous, Superstitious, Carnal, Proud, Wanton, Unclean, Mocking and Persecuting . . . return, return, believe and obey this Light."

William Penn made his point, with what he called "Apostolik blows and kicks"—vulgarly, often coarsely and arrogantly, "with lively cursing and rantings." His biographers use those and harder terms. *Truth Exalted,* so they write, is on the "low and muddy level of popular controversy," "the worst kind of religious" rant. It is "violent," "malicious," "abusive," without "humor, courtesy, dignity, or grace," and "a surprising disregard of good manners [and] Quakerly gentleness." It is the "noisy taunting . . . of a bawling fanatical Quaker, distressingly uncouth" (Vulliamy, *William Penn,* 1934). Penn made his point; with little of what his contemporary Lord Clarendon called "a flowing goodness."

Four months later, for the last time, Pepys wrote of Penn. On the evening of February 12, 1669, when he and his wife came home late, he found that Pelling, apothecary, "hath got me W. Pen's book against the Trinity. I got my wife to read it to me; and I find it so well writ as, I think, it is too good for him ever to have writ it; and it is a serious sort of book, and not fit for everybody to read." This, Penn's third pamphlet, was *The Sandy Foundation Shaken.* In it Penn wrote against the usual doctrine of the Trinity, against "The impossibility of God's pardoning sinners, without a plenary satisfaction," and against election. After the pamphlet had been issued, William Penn was sent to the Tower and stood in danger of being transported; chiefly, however, because he had not licensed the book with the Bishop of London. The pamphlet, Pepys thought, was controversial but restrained and clearly reasoned.

John Evelyn, to whom William Penn was only a name, gives in his Diary two lines which seem the verdict of seventeenth-century society. It is his only mention of Penn, and it comes between trivial facts—the text of the last Sunday's sermon and his having lately seen "a tall gigantic woman who measured 6 feet 10 inches." Evelyn's entry for January 3, is "About this time one of Sr. William Penn's sons had published a blasphemous book against the Deity of our Blessed Lord."

* * * * * *

William Penn wrote in 1673 his short explanation for becoming a Quaker after he had lived twenty years as an aristocrat. "And though I was a While in the Midst of this World's Glories, both in this and other Countries, yet it was rather to know, [so] that I might the better condemn them with a *Vanity of Vanities* . . . than to sit down and to be married with them. At last my Soul meeting with TRUTH . . . I embrac'd it with Gladness of Heart." *(Letter to Mary Pennyman* in 1673, Joseph Besse, 1726, Vol. I, p. 160).

It is a fact that at twenty-two Penn seemed an aristocrat; and it is a fact that at twenty-four he was completely a Quaker.

Three persons each had his explanation of the change. To Penn, his explanation seemed natural and complete, and it is transparently true to faith. Pepys assumed—nothing else ever entered his mind—that William Penn enjoyed his Paris clothes and his sword and his elegance. Some one else said that Penn let his conviction of 1673 write his explanation for 1664. Probably there is truth in each of these, complete truth in none. ("What is truth? said jesting Pilate.")

In any person, a great change may come sharply. It is time which proves the quality and power of the change, and its value. Time tryeth truth. What caused the change in Penn is an interesting inquiry, puzzling and human and valuable, but it is outside the immediate fact. It is not negligible; rather, it belongs in another category—abstract analysis. Only the new way of living counted in his life. Analysis of the cause of a change has its own purpose and reaches its own ends. Besides, why a man lives as he does may be as impossible to explain as why a poem is written.

Lady Penn

The only certain description of Lady Penn is the one Pepys wrote after he first saw her, August 19, 1664. "At noon dined at home, and after dinner my wife and I to Sir W. Pen's, to see his Lady, the first time, who is a well-looked, fat, short, old Dutchwoman, but one that hath been heretofore pretty handsome, and is now very discreet, and, I believe, hath more wit than her husband. Here we staid talking a good while, and very well pleased I was with the old woman at first visit." Old for a woman, meant any age past twenty-five; Lady Penn was probably two or three years past forty. She had been in Ireland managing their estate, a difficult matter. Her young son, Richard, had been with her. Her other son came home from his Grand Tour ten days after she was in London.

Pepys and his wife and the Penns (except after the first two months, young William Penn) were often together. They visited, and dined and supped together, and gossiped ("twatling at my Lady Pen's," Pepys calls it), and the women went buying, and all of them walked and went upon the river and in Sir William's coach to the open country outside the City. Pepys does not write that they sang together or went often to a play. They seemed to have liked being next-door neighbors. In the last four years of the Diary, Pepys names Lady Penn sixty times, never at length. She was part of the customary life. He keeps pretty much his first opinion of her, but being himself he fills it in.

To the last of the Diary, any meal he had at Lady Penn's offended him. Its meagerness and thin quality and the "dirty dishes" of its serving soured him to acid writing. Every dinner the Penns ate with him "hath been worth four of" theirs. Her "sorry" food—once "venison: baked in pans"—was no match for the elegance of his silver and the fulness of his meal, "served so nobly in plate, and a neat dinner, indeed, though but of seven dishes" (January 4, 1667). When he wrote he had supped with the Penns, he explained: "supped . . . that is eat some butter and radishes . . . not eating any other of their victuals which I hate because of their sluttery." That was the only fault he found lasting in Lady Penn.

Except her slovenly cooking, Pepys saw no defect in her housekeeping. At least he passed it with no outbursts. He was pleased by the novelty of her "fishes kept in a glass of water, that will live so for ever, and finely marked they are, being foreign" (May 28,

107

1665). She had judgment and taste when she and Elizabeth Pepys went buying. Pepys did gossip with Mrs. Turner and Sir William Batten about her husband and her son, William, and, though seldom, put a sharp point to the thrust of a sentence about her, but she held steadily in all he wrote of her his respect and liking, true if not strong.

She had a heavy taste in humor, but so had most of the seventeenth century. Pepys shows no distaste for her strong fun. One afternoon he went "to my Lady Batten's, [and] there found a great many women with her, in her chamber merry, my Lady Pen and her daughter, among others; where my Lady Pen flung me down upon the bed, and herself and others, one after another, upon me, and very merry we were" (April 12, 1665). The evening of the Day of Thanksgiving for victory over the Dutch, Pepys asked Lady Penn and Peg and others (Sir William was with the fleet) to a "venison pasty." They supped, and till about twelve at night they were "flinging our fireworks, . . . abundance of serpents and rockets . . . and burning one another and people over the way." In the house, Lady Penn and the rest all were "mighty merry, smutting one another with candle grease and soot, till most of us were like devils." About one o'clock they went to Pepys's house and had wine and danced and dressed up, Pepys and one other man as women; "my wife and Pegg Pen put on perriwigs" . . . and one woman danced a jigg. "Thus we spent till three or four in the morning mighty merry," (August 14, 1666).

All this seems less strange when read with the memory of the parlor games played then and later: blindman's buff, with its merry bruisings (buff was a word for hit); London bridge, that ended in a tug of war; crack the whip, which might cripple; hot cockles, the point of which was one player's batting another as hard as he wanted to; and other sports needing to play them right much punching and slapping with soot-blackened hands. Pepys did not care for this fun. The day after Christmas, 294 years ago, Pepys, who had been from home "all the afternoon and evening till late, . . . stepped in" to see his wife, as he went to his office. He found "my people and wife innocently at cards very merry," and he went on to his office, "leaving them to their sport and blindman's buff." He did not go back to them again for their sport. He went to bed.

Lady Penn and Dicke held his liking much more than anyone else in the family. She stayed in his grace; Sir William never entered it. When Pepys, one evening in 1667, was at Sir William's with "his Lady and Pegg and pretty Mrs. Lowther her Peg's sister-in-law ... Sir W. Pen, half drunk, did talk like a fool and vex his wife, that I was half pleased and half vexed [for Lady Penn, one supposes] to see so much folly and rudeness from him" (May 28). He never saw folly or rudeness in Lady Penn. After Peg's marriage, a sourness came for a while into what he wrote of her. Yet only once, even in an aside, does he turn a sharp phrase to Lady Penn. Once, ten days after the wedding, she sinks, in his exasperation at her "great content," with the marriage to "that silly woman." (Feb. 24, 1667).

The most generous writing Pepys did about any of the Penns was about young Richard, who was nine or ten when he came from Ireland with his mother. It was a pleasant custom—strong with Pepys and his wife—for a lady on Valentine's Eve to name someone as her Valentine. In 1665, Mrs. Pepys named Dicke. So, February 14, "This morning [while Pepys and Mrs. Pepys were still in bed] comes betimes Dicke Pen, to be my wife's Valentine, and come to our bedside. By the same token, I had him brought to my side, thinking to make him kiss me; but he perceived me, and would not." Dicke preferred to kiss his Valentine and so he went to her: "a notable, stout, witty boy." He died at eighteen.

Peg and Anthony Lowther, a young wealthy gentleman, were married in February, 1667. The wedding was private: "no friends, but two or three relatives on his side and hers." Pepys and Elizabeth Pepys had not been invited, though the Penns "Borrowed many things from my kitchen for dressing the dinner." Pepys saw a slight put upon him in giving out the wedding favors. So for a while he defined Peg with her father; and her husband, who a month before had been "a pretty gentleman" (January 4, 1667), became his subject for libelous gossip. The Lowthers were in Pepys's milder phrasing "a very sorry couple ... though rich": he had a bad body and an evil temper, and she was silly and proud and unmannerly. Pepys collected faults about them, largely from Mrs. Turner. Four months after the wedding Sir William Batten, ancient and garrulous, told Pepys "how Mrs. Lowther had her train held up yesterday by her page at his house in the country; which is so ridiculous a piece of pride as I am ashamed of" (June 28, 1667). Later that year (September 11, 1667) Pepys and his wife gave the two "an extraordinary good and handsome dinner ... better than they deserve or understand." Pepys that day wrote Peg down as "grown ... a beggarly, proud fool," with her silences at the dinner, her "gold coach," her "bracelet of diamonds and rubies about her wrist, and a sixpenny necklace ... and not one good rag of clothes to her back." He broke "up the company soon as [he] could; not much mirth."

* * * * * *

A Sunday in July the same year, Pepys, his wife, and Mrs. Turner drove down to Epsom in a coach and four. On the way, he and Mrs. Turner talked over with pleasure the pride and ignorance of Mrs. Lowther; in special, her "having her train carried up." Lady Penn was no part of such talk. It was a happy day of high English summer. They were away from Seething Lane soon after five o'clock in the morning; "The country very fine"; "a breeze abroad"; trees were still full-leaved; the fields were green, and in one near Epsom were sheep and an old shepherd with sheep crook and dog, to whom his young son was reading the Bible. Pepys listened, and had the boy read to him. (He read in "the forced tone that children do usually read"); and he said to the shepherd that the boy read well. The father thanked Pepys and said he did bless God for his boy. He told Pepys that he earned 4 shillings a week the year round and that he had 18 score of sheep to mind. The downs were full of small stones, and Pepys "tried to cast stones with the shepherd's crooke." They talked of the old dog, which the shepherd valued, for he "would turn sheep any way" the shepherd wished, "to folde them." Pepys "took notice of the shepherd's shoes, shod with iron . . . both at the toe and heels," which, the shepherd said, "will make the stones fly till they sing before me." It was to Pepys a world of innocence. The shepherd was "the most like one of the old patriarchs that ever I saw . . . and it brought . . . thoughts of the old age of the world in my mind for two or three days after." In "the field [they] gathered one of the prettiest nosegays that ever I saw," and they "stopped a . . . woman with her milk-pail and . . . did drink our belly-fulls of milk, better than any cream." When the sun was down they started, with pleasure, in the cool of the evening, for home. "Anon it grew dark, and as it grew dark" there were fireflies, "which was mighty pretty." They got home at eleven o'clock; "Thanks to God no business happened in my absence." Pepys could compass contrasts of mood and strange oppositions of spirit, as he did that day.

* * * * * *

The last entry about Lady Penn, made eight months before the Diary ends, gives in a quiet action Penn's lasting feeling toward her and Sir William. Toward both of them it is much what it had been four years earlier when he first saw Lady Penn. September 22, 1668, he was "Up and to the Office all the morning"; then dinner; and then "to the Office again . . . busy all the afternoon"; and all the evening he was walking in the dark, in the garden, "to favour my eyes, which I find nothing but ease to help." Into "the garden there comes to me my Lady Penn, . . . and we sat and talked together, and he went with her to her house and there eat a bit of something, and by and by comes Sir W. Pen, and eat with us, and mighty merry—in appearance at least, he being on all occasions glad to be at friendship with me, though we hate one another, and knew it on both sides. They gone . . . I to walk in the garden." After his busy and troubled day, he wrote a quiet account in quiet style.

The next May, when the Diary ends, relations still stand as they did the year before. Whatever Pepys wrote of Sir William held the essence of enmity; Peg—almost always "Mrs. Lowther" after her marriage—attracted him and seemed ready to be kind to him, and being married should, he thinks, be able to look out for herself. Lady Penn increasingly was as she has been the five years he has known her.

Lady Penn, the Diary and the writings of William Penn show, was a good mother and a good wife, a pleasant woman, vigorous, practical, alert, even, with much sense and kindness and force. The kitchen gossip of Mrs. Turner can be disregarded. The year of her birth is not known. The eighteenth anniversary of her wedding Sir William was celebrated in January, 1662. Her given name was Margaret, her family name is said to have been Jasper. Her marriage entry in St. Martin Ludgate reads "widow." Her nationality, whether she was Dutch or Irish, and where she was born and brought up are not surely known. In fact, except for what Pepys says of her, most comments about her are conjectures.

PEPYS'S SONGS

In the Diary, Pepys tells that he composed the music for four songs. *Composed* seems to mean he wrote the melody and some one else wrote part or all the accompaniment.

The entry for January 30, 1660—the first month of the Diary—begins: "This morning, before I was up, I fell a-singing of my song, 'Great, good, and just,' &c.,' and put myself thereby in mind that this was the fatal day, now ten years since, his Majesty died." [It was eleven "years since."] That song, written before the Diary, Pepys does not speak of again. Its words are the first eight lines of verses by the Marquis of Montrose on the execution of Charles:

> Great, good, and just, could I but rate
> My grief and thy too rigid fate,
> I'd weep the world to such a strain
> That it should deluge once again.
> But since thy loud-tongued blood demands supplies
> More from Briareus' hands, than Argus' eyes,
> I'll sing thy obsequies with trumpet sounds,
> And write thy epitaph with blood and wounds.

Montrose was the King's chief general in Scotland. In 1650—in his thirties — he was beheaded for his loyalty to Charles. To the Royalists he was a romantic hero and a martyr. A few of his lyrics are excellent. His best-known lines are in *I'll Never Love Thee More:* "He either fears his fate too much,/ Or his deserts are small,/ That dares not put it to the touch,/ To gain or lose it all."

Gaze not on Swans was Pepys second song. The evening of February 11, 1662, though his mind was full of improving his garden and "getting things in the office settled to the advantage of my clerks," he began to make a song of his own. The words were by Henry Noel, a writer so obscure that the DNB prints no life of him and the *Cambridge History of English Literature* gives only, as does the DNB, that he and four other young gentlemen of the

112

Inner Temple (Christopher Hatton, later Lord Chancellor, was one) in 1568, wrote *Gismond of Salerne*, each writing an act, Noel, the second, 246 lines. Noel died in 1596. The play as first written is a Senecan tragedy; is in verse rhymed *abab;* is based on a Boccaccio tale, which is turned into almost a Morality; is short— about 1600 lines; and a prefatory sonnet to the play tells was acted before the Queen "by the pleasant side/ of famous Thames at Grenwich." (The original *Gismond of Salerne* is in Cunliffe's *Early English Classic Tragedies.*) Henry Lawes (1595-1662) had published *Gaze not on Swans* set to his own music in the first issue of his *Ayres and Dialogues,* 1653. Lawes was one of the best and best-known composers and publishers of music in his time. Charles I appointed him a Gentleman of the Chapel Royal and a member of the King's band. Under the Commonwealth he was music-tutor in the family of the Earl of Bridgewater, at Ludlow Castle, and he chose *Comus* (Milton then was only twenty-six) and directed it and composed music for it and played the Attendant Spirit in it when it was given for the first time, in 1634, at Ludlow Castle. In 1656 he wrote music for Davenant's *Entertainment.* When the King came back, Lawes made an anthem for the Coronation, and he was appointed again to his offices in the Chapel Royal. Milton wrote a sonnet which praised him; Herrick, too, wrote a poem to "My Harrie"; and "in the first edition of Herrick, Waller, . . . Carew, and others, it is mentioned that Lawes set some of their words to music" (DNB), to which music the poets gave "admiration."

Poets of the English Language, v.II, Auden and Pearson, prints *Swans* as being attributed to William Strode, an Oxford writer, 1600-1645. Bertram Dobell in his *The Poetical Works of William Strode,* 1907, prints it under *Doubtful Pieces* ("They may be his"). He explains: "The only authority for attributing the lines . . . to Strode, is that the poem is mentioned in Dr. Grosart's list of his poems (Dobell, p.122) . . . I do not know on what authority Dr. Grosart attributed it to Strode, but I suppose he had seen some MS. in which it was assigned to him. (p.129) . . . Lawes' *Ayres and Dialogues*" . . . assigned [it] to Henry Noel, who would seem therefore to have the best claim to it (p.122) Dr. Grosart was not an ideal editor; . . . much of his work needs to be done again by more . . . critical hands (li)." Dr. Alexander B. Grosart 1827-1899, edited 130 volumes of Elizabethan and Jacobian literature.

There might, too, be doubt that Strode was capable of the poetic taste. When Orpheus sang of Euridice's death, Strode wrote

> The trees to heare
> Obtayn'd an eare,
> And after left it off againe.

Noel's lyric begins, in Lawes's spelling (Latter from the Library of Congress):

> Gaze not on Swanns in whose soft brest
> A full hatcht beauty seems to nest;
> Nor snow which falling from the skye,
> Hovers in its virginity.

Then, for two stanzas, we are told not to gaze on roses, or on "Lillies which no subtle Bee/ Hath rob'd by Kissing Chymistry," or the milky way, or "Pearle whose silver walls confine/ The Riches of an Indian Mine."

> For [the fourth stanza says] if my Emp'ress appears,
> Swanns moultring dye, snow melts to tears,
> Roses do blush and hang their heads,
> Pale Lillies shrink into their beds.

Stanzas five and six repeat the idea, circle about, return, and the song ends. The verse is musical, and it moves with lightness and gaiety and much charm. It trips its measure of melody. The pattern of the first three stanzas, each opening with "Gaze not on," is a pleasant repeating form used in sixteenth and seventeenth century lyrics. Carew's *Ask Me No More* is the best of such lyrics.

Two weeks after Pepys began the song he finished it, on the day after "by God's mercy I am 29 years of age, and in very good health, and like to live and get an estate; and . . . I think I may reckon myself as happy a man as any is in the world, for which God be praised."

For six weeks before that, he had been taking lessons in the composition of music from Mr. Thomas Berkenshaw, an established musician and teacher. "That rare artist," Evelyn called him after hearing him play, (August 3, 1664). "I am resolved," Pepys had written in January, the thirteenth, "to begin to learn of him to compose, and to begin tomorrow, he giving me good hopes I shall soon do it." Pepys did begin the next day, and kept on until February 27, though he thought 5 pounds for a month or five weeks was "a great deal of money" and was troubled at parting with it. After he had finished *Swans* and Mr. Berkenshaw had copied it for him, Pepys decided he had all the rules Mr. Berkenshaw could teach and it was "not good for me to continue with him at £5 a month." (Henry Lawes had been paid £1. s.10 pound a week for

114

teaching Lady Dering.) Pepys paid him on the twenty-fourth and stopped his lessons; and they parted with some angry words over Mr. Berkenshaw's certainty that his rules of composition were perfect. Pepys thought they were good and the best that ever were made, but not perfect. He set the rules down that day in fair order in a book; he was at it all the morning.

Mr. Berkenshaw taught Pepys by giving him rules for composition, by setting him words to make a melody to and talking over the melody Pepys had written, and sometimes by writing his own melody for the words to show Pepys what the rules meant and how best to apply them.

Pepys liked his song. The day he ended it he found it pleased him very much, and three weeks later, when he played it on his lute in the evening, he still found it "incomparable" and was "not a little proud of it." Besides, no one else in the world had it. Even Mr. Berkenshaw kept no copy.

Pepys's third song was *Beauty Retire,* eight lines from Davenant's *The Siege of Rhodes* (End of Act IV, Part II) set to his own melody.

Solymon. Beauty, retire! Thou dost my pitty move!
Believe my pitty, and then trust my love!—
(Exit Roxalana)

At first I thought her by our prophet sent
As a reward for valours toils,
More worth than all my fathers spoils:
And now, she is become my punishment.
But thou are just, O Pow'r Divine!
With new and painfull arts
Of study'd warr I break the hearts
Of half the world, and she breaks mine.
(Exit)

On Wednesday, December 6, 1665, Pepys first wrote of this song: "it being fast day . . . I spent the afternoon upon a song of Solyman's words to Roxalana, that I have set"; and toward evening he and his wife walked to the beautiful Mrs. Pierce's. Others came there—and among them, Mrs. Coleman, the singer, and "my dear Mrs. Knipp," and the lady "with her singing daughter." They all sang. What Pepys wrote of that evening is some measure of the intense feeling music gave him: "Here the best company for musique I ever was in, in my life, and wish I could live and die in it, both for the musique and the face of Mrs. Pierce, and my wife and Knipp, who is pretty enough; . . . I spent the night in

115

extasy almost." After three days the song was finished and he sang it to Mr. Thomas Hill, the merchant, who loved music and came to Pepys "a 'Sundays, a most ingenious and sweet-natured and highly accomplished person," whom, twenty years later, Pepys still wrote of as his friend.

A month after that, January 3, 1666, in "a good company" at Pepys's house, Mrs. Coleman, who had sung the heroine Ianthe in *The Siege of Rhodes, Part One,* "sang my words I set to *Beauty Retire,* and I think it is a good song, and they praise it mightily. Mrs. Coleman sang very finely, though her voice was decayed as to strength but mighty sweet though soft, and a pleasant jolly woman."

Pepys kept taking pleasure in his song. February 23, 1666, his thirty-third birthday, he was teaching it to his wife, "which she sings and makes go most rarely, and a very fine song it seems to be." The next day he worked at his office till three o'clock, much past his dinner time, and then at home as he said "eat a bite alone, my wife being gone out." In the afternoon, with Mr. Hill, he went by coach to Hayle's, the painter's, to meet his wife and Mrs. Pierce and Mrs. Knipp. "Here we had ale and cakes . . . and [Mrs. Knipp] sung my song, which she now sings bravely, and makes me proud of myself."

Six months later, well on in August of 1666, a crowded year for Pepys, *Beauty Retire* still pleased him when he had time to think of it. Mrs. Knipp told him his song was "mightily cried up, which I am not a little proud of." Then, September 2, came the Great Fire; yet in November Pepys and Mrs. Knipp sang the song to the company at Mrs. Pierce's, and again Pepys was sure "without flattery . . . it is good in its kind." For the last time *Beauty Retire* enters the Diary on December 4, 1666, a year after Pepys wrote it. He went home that noon and "Goodgroome dined with us, who teaches my wife to sing. After dinner I did give him my song, *Beauty Retire,* which he has often desired of me, and without flattery, I think is a very good song."

The song fades from the Diary on this happy conviction.

John Goodgroome was a composer and a violinist and a teacher, whom Pepys much respected. He became one of the King's "twenty-four Fiddlers at the Chapel Royal."

Beauty Retire is largely recitative as the Restoration defined that term. Recitative is musical talk, musical declamation, fairly new in England, fitted like a good part of *The Siege of Rhodes* to give the meaning and measure of speech within a relatively small range

116

of notes. It is an opposite to the florid arabesques of French and Italian arias. Pepys is not a genius on song-writing. *Beauty Retire* is a pleasant song: "an excellent song..., which is very much more than the dilletante achievement of an accomplished amateur" (Sir Arthur Bryant, *Pepys*).

The last song Pepys wrote of in the Diary is *It is Decreed,* a melody with words by Ben Jonson. Part of Jonson's lines are: "It is decreed—nor shall thy fate, O Rome!/ Resist my vow, though hills were set on hills." He began it about April 5, 1666; that evening he went "home and late putting notes to *It is decreed, nor shall thy fate, etc.* and then to bed." He did not finish this "ayre"— the unaccompanied melody—until the second week in November, the eleventh.

In the seven months from April to November, he often had his song in mind. He ends a long and crowded entry for April 18: "In all my ridings in the coach and intervals my mind hath been full these three weeks of setting in musique *It is decreed, etc.*" And three months later after he had waited all day for news from the English fleet which was fighting the Dutch off the south coast, he wrote, "I home, and there after a little while making of my tune to *It is decreed,* to bed" (July 27, 1666).

Even when the song, "my new recitative," was down he did not until a month later (December 10), what with the Dutch war, get to writing his accompaniment. When he had written it, it seems not to have pleased him; for ten days afterward as he came from Whitehall he met Mr. Hingston, a musician and his old friend, and took him to the Dog Tavern, showed him the song, and asked him to write "a base." Mr. Hingston read the music, and said the air was good and "the words plainly expressed," and he would write the bass. Pepys was pleased—mightily. Mr. Hingston was an older man than Pepys, an honored composer and organist, who had served Charles I and Cromwell and Charles II, and in 1666 was a Gentleman of the Chapel Royal and Keeper of the Organs. He had been taught by Orlando Gibbons and had taught John Blow. At the tavern that day they talked until well toward noon, and finding they agreed on many matters they separated with mutual esteem.

On Christmas Day, Pepys had the accompaniment from Mr. Hingston; he was pleased—again mightily. More than ever he liked his song, and for his and their pleasure he taught it to his wife, to her two women, Mercer and Barker; and since just then he could not teach it to the unmatchable Mrs. Knipp, he taught

117

it to John Harris, the chief actor in Davenant's company of the Duke's Playhouse. The manuscript of *It is Decreed* is at Cambridge.

Pepys took almost ten months to write this song, for many important things were using his time and his energy—a fear that the Plague of 1665 was starting again; the Great Fire, which nearly burned his home and his office and quite upset for months his life at each of these, as it quite upset all the rest of London; the battle between Parliament and the Admiralty; the Dutch naval war, in which Pepys had a central responsibility; his "great letter to the Duke of York," at the writing of which (in "foule shorthand") he worked steadily from a little past noon till midnight one day, and "which do lay the ill condition of the Navy ... open to him" and showed the need of "money to carry on the war, before it be too late, or else lay out for a peace upon any termes" (November 1, 1666). Pepys's year was crowded, yet he finished his song.

PROSE OF THE DIARY

Music is a constant topic in the Diary. Often for awhile the Diary lets music lie unseen below what is told of acts and personalities, yet it soon comes again into expression, for Pepys's interest in music never ended. He writes of his own singing and composing and playing; of listening to the singing and playing of others; of choosing a servant partly because he had a good voice or read music or played the lute; of teaching his wife and his friends and his servants to sing; of studying the science of music— its structure, theory, mathematics; of speculating whether music-charts and other like inventions—were ever a help in composition; of going to hear good music and of his delight when he was surprised by good music heard unexpectedly. At home early and late, and at his friends'; at sea and on the Thames going down to inspect a Shipyard; in his own or in somebody else's garden; at church; at inns and taverns; and in coaches as he traveled on business; in almost every place and in most conditions of mind, Pepys sang or played or heard music, or he talked of it, or read or thought of it. He himself had a pleasant, well-trained voice, and played with skill the flageolet, the lute, and the treble viol. One June evening "it being very hot weather I took my flageolette and played upon the leads [the flat roof of his house] in the garden, where Sir. W. Pen came out in his shirt onto his leads, and there we staid talking and singing, and drinking great drafts of claret, and eating botargo [fish roe "to promote drinking"] and bread and butter till twelve at night, it being moonshine; and so to bed, very near fuddled" (June 5, 1661). There are many such entries, with variations.

Some kinds of music Pepys did not care for, though his interest included most. In general, he liked the sort he heard at the theaters or at Court or in the King's Chapel and the Queen's, more than he liked traditional ballads or the simplicity of earlier religious music. He did, though, like the zest and gaiety and salt of glees and jigs and catches, and of some old-fashioned country tunes.

He had an investigative interest—almost a scientist's—in the new music at Whitehall and at St. James's, yet he did not accept that new fashion imported from France or Italy because it was new and the fashion of the Court. His taste determined his verdict.

His delight in the music he enjoyed was intense. After hearing Massinger's *The Virgin Martyr,* he wrote:

"A ... not that the play is worth much. ... But that which did please me beyond any thing in the whole world was the wind-musique when the angel comes down, which is so sweet that it ravished me, and indeed, in a word, did wrap up my soul so that it made me really sick, just as I have formerly been when in love with my wife; that neither then, nor all the evening going home, and at home, I was able to think of any thing, but remained all night transported, so as I could not believe that ever any musick hath that real command over the soul of a man as this did upon me" (27 February 1668).

Pepys was not, of course, all music. So far as we know, he did not sing at his work or fiddle in office time. He was an officer of the Admiralty and enjoyed his work. He gave great energy to it and kept studying day after day to do it better; and he did keep on doing better. When he became Clerk of the Acts he knew almost nothing about his work. He could not tell one kind of timber from another. And he had never learned the multiplication table, but not knowing it he got up at four o'clock in the morning and learned it. Though at first he did not understand any of the minutiae of his office, later he planned and built—with zigzags of success and failure—an English Navy which for a little while fore-shadowed the Navy of Nelson. Yet all the time music was a good companion, which he left only for awhile and then came back to.

* * * * * *

Almost nothing has been written about the music in Pepys's prose, about its style. The prose of the Diary is admirable. Rhythms (accents heavy and light, and pauses), the sounds of vowels and consonants in the phrasing, the variety and length and arrange-ment of phrases and sentences and words, all mingle into a fluid whole as the different ideas and feelings follow one another. The reader, unless he is an analyst, does not notice what makes the effect nor does it seem to him that Pepys ever was consciously after an effect. Indeed, Pepys wrote spontaneously; he wrote as he did because he thought and felt as he did and had a great literary gift. Pepys—to put it another way—was absorbed by the facts and by his feelings about them, and he could write prose that carried the facts and the implications, the suggestion, the experience which the facts had for him. His prose has the resonance of his temperament, his character, his abilities. His prose is his personality expressing itself in words.

When he tells a matter dull for him, it becomes dull stuff from the style of telling; when he tells a happy matter, his writing gets the happiness. His Navy Office summaries are sharply business-like; his excitement about a good play carries excitement.

The first Sunday he went to Saint Olave's after the Plague, Pepys walked through the churchyard (326, dead from the Plague, were buried there and in the church). "It frighted me indeed... more than I thought it could have done, to see so [many] graves lie so high upon the churchyards where people have been buried of the plague. ... I ... do not think to go through it again a good while" (January 30, 1666).

In the evening, September 2, 1666, the first day of the Great Fire, Pepys, watching from "a little ale-house on the Bankside... saw the fire grow ... more and more ..., in corners and upon steeples, and between churches and houses, as far as we could see up the hill of the City, in a most horrid malicious bloody flame, not like the fine flame of an ordinary fire ..., it made me weep to see it. The churches, houses, and all on fire and flaming at once, and a horrid noise the flames made, and the cracking of houses at their ruins."

In both these, Pepys tells of his fear. The first holds an ominous, almost unlocalised feeling of horror, which Pepys implies but does not name; the second tells his specific terror of the Fire, with specific terms. In the first, the phrases are longer and slower-moving, and heavy with m's and n's and lagging ld's, d's, k's, and t's. The second has shorter phrases and sharper, higher sounds which run on faster.

One meal which Pepys had with the Duke of Albermarle, he did not enjoy: "I find the Duke of Albermarle at dinner with sorry company, some of his officers of the Army; dirty dishes, and a nasty wife at table, and bad meat, at which I made but an ill dinner" (4 April, 1667). In one sentence, three lines of the Diary, Pepys makes the facts quite clear. He gives, too, his feeling, by jagged phrases chopped into short lengths, by omitting many "and's," by the sound of the words "sorry," "dirty," "nasty," by

121

strong alliteration of sharp "t's" and "d's." Pepys had been irritated by this dinner and still was irritated as he wrote those uncomfortable rhythms and the jangled sounds.

Sunday, June 11, 1665, Pepys had quite another sort of meal: "In the evening comes Mr. Andrews and his wife and Mr. Hill, and stayed and played, and sung and supped, most excellent pretty company, so pleasant, ingenious, and harmless, I cannot desire better. They gone we to bed, my mind in great present ease" (Vol. 4, p. 407). Mr. Andrews was Pepys's friend before the Diary starts, and Mr. Hill he met in 1664 and kept as a good friend long after the Diary ends. What he says of the supper has a pervading sense of ease and comfort and rest among old friends, stated in clear facts and sustained in the simplest kind of sentence built upon parallel phrases linked in many "and's." The writing never rises to any sharp description. It flows slowly, yet it never drags because it has in it clear open vowels and liquid consonants —l, m, n, r—and alliteration, and almost rhyming words. Toward the end of the first sentence, the words become longer and more homely; they move on slowly: "excellent pretty company, so pleasant, ingenious, and harmless." The second sentence, which ends the account, is contrastingly short. It shows two moods. The first phrases of five words—bare, short, clipped—tells that the evening is done: "They gone we to bed." The rhythm and sound of the next six words—the last six—carry the earlier mood.

One afternoon, May 22, when he was thirty, he walked with John Creed, secretary of the Tangier Commission, from Greenwich to Woolwich, down along the river, four miles or so. He wrote "... by water to Greenwich, and [after] calling at the little alehouse at the end of the town to wrap a rag about my little left toe, [it] being new sore with walking, we walked pleasantly to Woolwich, in our way hearing the nightingales sing." He seems to have written this off-hand. In the half-sentence he gives, quite completely and quite without strain, the tone of the pleasure he had on the walk. He uses short words, innocently actual details, barely two adjectives, a child-like directness of phrasing, and the nightingale for poetry and wonder.

Two long quotations, one from the Diary, the other from a letter, are fair examples of wholly different tones in Pepys's writing. The first was written when he was about thirty-two: "... To the 'Change after office, and received my watch from the watchmaker, and a very fine [one] it is, given me by Briggs, the Scrivener. ... But, Lord! to see how much of my old folly and childishnesse

122

hangs upon me still that I cannot forbear carrying my watch in my hand in the coach all this afternoon, and seeing what o'clock it is one hundred times, and am apt to think with myself, how could I be so long without one; though I remember since, I had one, and found it a trouble, and resolved to carry one no more about me while I lived. So home to supper and to bed" (May 13, 1665).

The second is from a letter to Evelyn, written when Pepys was sixty-seven and living in leisure at Clapham. "I have no herds to mind, nor will my Doctor allow me any books here. What, then, ... you say, ... are you doing? Why, truly, nothing that will bear naming, and yet I am not, I think, idle; for who can, that has so much of past and to come to think on, as I have? And thinking, I take it, is working, though many forms beneath what my Lady and you are doing. But pray remember what o'clock it is with you and me; and be not now, by overstirring, too bold with your present complaint, any more that I dare be with mine, which, too, has been no less kind in giving me my warning, than the other to you, and to neither of us, I hope, and, through God's mercy, dare say, either unlooked for or unwelcome. I wish, nevertheless, that I were able to administer any thing towards the lengthening that precious rest of life which God has thus long blessed you, and, in you, mankind, with; but I have always been too little regardful of my own health, to be a prescriber to others...." Chapham, 7 August, 1700.

* * * * * *

In the beginning God created the heaven and the earth. And the earth was without form, and void; and darkness was upon the face of the deep. And the Spirit of God moved upon the face of the waters. And God said, Let there be light: and there was light. And God saw the light, that it was good: and God divided the light from the darkness. And God called the light Day, and the darkness he called Night. And the evening and the morning were the first day. Genesis I, 1-5.

The Diary was written in an age of great prose. Within, roughly, the hundred and fifty years after 1550, the Book of Common Prayer (1549, 1552) and the King James Bible were published, and North's Plutarch (1579), Donne's devotional prose, Shakespeare, Bacon's *Essays*, Sir Thomas Browne's *Religio Medici*, and much of Milton and Dryden and Fuller and Izaak Walton and

Bunyan and others. This English prose had pungency and exactness and comprehensibility, color and beauty and surprise. Unlike earlier writing in English it gave no implied or open apology for not being Latin or Greek. The new science, too, thought English a good language. In 1667 the Royal Society, which Pepys had become a member of in 1665, urged that writers and speakers reject all "swellings of style," that they aim at "a close, naked, natural way of speaking . . . a native ease," and, above all, that they use the speech of common men.

Pepys knew the classics, and much of the best writing of the closer past and of his own time. He valued the older, established writers. Contemporary writing he judged as he did any other sort of work by men he knew. He went to many plays of Dryden ("Dryden the poet I knew at Cambridge"; February 3, 1662), who was about his own age, some of which he cared for not at all and some of which, he wrote, "pleased me mightily." And he read Dryden's prose and did not hesitate to give his opinions of it. "I bought the Mayden Queen, a play newly printed which I like, at the King's house so well. . . . Mr. Dryden, . . . he himself, in his preface, seems to brag of [it] and indeed it is a good play" (January 18, 1668). He suggested to Dryden putting Chaucer's *Poor Person* into contemporary verse. Thomas Fuller, twenty-five years older than Pepys, he knew so well that when he "met with Dr. Thomas Fuller" he "took him to The Dog, where he did tell me of his last and great book which is coming out: that is, his History of all the Families in England; and he could tell me more of my own than I knew myself" (January 22, 1661). Once he had a long talk with Fuller about ways of writing, and another time he heard Fuller preach. It was "a dry sermon." Pepys looked at Dryden and Fuller and other writers of his time with a level eye, seeing them not magnified or lessened by distance and accumulated criticism.

The two books Pepys read and heard and valued most were the King James Bible and the Book of Common Prayer. The Diary shows this all through it, in big things and little. The Bible, with the Prayer Book, has changing and suitable rhythms, gained it seemed unconsciously; it uses exact and simple words; it prefers to be specific rather than to generalize; and the subject is always clearly dominant, made all the more so by being written of in prose beautifully suited to express it. Such prose, the seventeenth century at its best valued and wrote; and so, at its best, seventeenth century prose has force and clearness and luminous suggestion. Izaak Walton and Sir Thomas Browne and John Bunyan and Pepys, in different styles, wrote that sort of prose. Browne, in the *Religio Medici,* quite individually wrote: "There is surely a piece of divinity in us, something that was before the elements, and owes no homage to the sun." And "We carry within us the wonders we seek without us; There is all Africa and her prodigies in us." And "We see by an invisible sun within us." Half way through "The Fourth Day" of the *Complete Angler* Walton wrote: "No life, my honest scholar, no life so happy and so pleasant as the life of a well-governed angler; for while the lawyer is swallowed up with business, and the statesman is preventing or contriving plots, then we sit on cowslip banks, hear the birds sing, and possess ourselves in as much quietness as those silent silver streams, which we now see glide so quietly by us." Bunyan, telling the death of Mr. Valiant-for-Truth, ended: "And so he passed over and all the trumpets sounded for him on the other side." "And the Pilgrim they laid in an upper chamber, whose windows opened toward the sun-rising: the name of the chamber was Peace; where he slept till break of day, and then he arose and sang." Browne, Walton, and Bunyan, each speaks in his own way, yet the Bible and the Prayer Book have a part in them all; as the two books have in the quite different writing of the Diary.

SIR WILLIAM DAVENANT

THE SIEGE OF RHODES

The Commonwealth closed the theatres—lewd vanities, a stench in the nostrils of the righteous. It discouraged, when it did not ban, public concerts of voices and instruments, and it ended, though not entirely, the music long established in cathedrals and great churches and foundations, and the pipings of village choirs. Yet Cromwell "loved a good singing, and instruments well played," especially organs and trumpets and strings. Bulstrode Whitelocke in his *Memorials* tells that Cromwell in private with him would "lay aside his greatness and write verse by way of diversion." It is said that he had a pleasant voice for singing and that at the marriage of his daughter Elizabeth he had forty-five violins to play.

Others high in the Puritan Party, because of taste and character and upbringing "even in these discordant times," played or sang or listened to music with pleasure. One of those was Bulstrode Whitelocke, M.P., Cromwell's Keeper of the Great Seal, a writer himself, and a close friend of Cromwell's, to whom harassed writers turned. At Oxford, when he was sixteen, "he recreated himself with music and field sports." Later, at the Middle Temple, he was Master of the Revels and once had "the whole care and charge of all the music of the great masque [given in 1626] which was so performed that it excelled all music that ever before that time had been heard in England." General Lord Fairfax, who the Speaker of the House said was made Commonwealth Commander-in-Chief for his "valour, conduct, and fidelity" was high and honorable and cultured, a student of Latin and fluent in Italian and French, a lover of flowers and maker of gardens, a verse writer if not a poet, a benefactor of Oxford, and an excellent landlord of his Yorkshire estate, "Nunappleton." He is credited with saving York Cathedral from being bombarded. ("To Fairfax belongs this praise," is a footnote in Evelyn's Diary.) Essex, another of Cromwell's chief generals (Robert Devereaux, Earl of Essex, son of Elizabeth's dazzling favorite), was like Whitelock and Fairfax, a man of culture.

There were others. Not all Commonwealth men believed it was commanded they smash the stained glass of Winchester Cathedral and the great organ of Exeter. Yet the extremists, the Men of Severity, felt sure that in this world pleasures were snares set by the devil and beauty a mockery, and that no moment was sanctified unless it was sour and arid from denial of natural joy. These men were strong in the Commonwealth.

The Commonwealth closed the theater not chiefly because the government was opposed to the drama as a form but because play-going brought too light-minded, too holiday, a mood; because immorality grew up around the playhouse; because of the evil tone of London plays and their scurrilities and "wanton jest"; because of the dangers to public safety and public health; and because of the spirit of riot latent in the undisciplined crowd. The playhouse, the Commonwealth had judged, "wronged Religion, Government, Safety, and Modestie."

Yet plays were given. Now and then "clandestine performances" did take place, though rarely and in disguise and with danger to the actors and the audience. In 1655, for instance, "during the Troubles," in "*one Mr. Gibbions his Tennis Court*," "the poor *Comoedians*" acting *Claracilla* "were *betrayed* to the authorities . . . [by] one of their fellows, an ill *Beest*, . . . causing the poor *Actors* to be routed by *Souldiery*." Some kinds of stage entertainments the government licensed. "Moral representation," much like the old pointed didactic moralities, were allowed to be put on privately by special groups, and tableaux and rich ceremonial masques sometimes could be given in schools and in the beautiful hall of the Inner Temple and at an embassy—the Portuguese for one. Often these were elaborate. A private entertainment, *Cupid and Death*, a masque by John Shirley "with Scenes and Musick, Vocall & Instrumentall," given by the Military Company, had elegance of scenery and acting, and it had music by Matthew Lock and Christopher Gibbons. In general, these allowed plays were sharply moralistic, even political propaganda; and being privately given and acted for the most part by amateurs, they were held to be uncontaminated. Strangely, tumbling and tightrope dancing and acrobatics, which had great and open popularity at country fairs and taverns and on village greens, were at times part of a polished London entertainment. The Indians of Peru, in Davenant's *Cruelty of the Spaniards,* climbed and leaped and tumbled, and the attendants of the Priest of the Sun delighted with their leapings and tumblings, and with "a double Somerset." Later *Macbeth* was "dressed" with "flying for the Witches" and "machines" and dances.

* * * * * *

The fortunes and misfortunes of Sir William Davenant (1601-1668) show fairly the course of the seventeenth century theater. Davenant wrote some of the best plays of his time, plays which followed the Elizabethan tradition rather than led into the Restoration. When he was twenty-two, in the third year of Charles I, he wrote a play which critics said showed "mastery of stagecraft," "a high quality of style," and even did "catch echoes of Shakespeare." It pleased the public and the King, and for the next years Davenant went on in favor with the King and with Queen Henrietta Maria and with the public.

A court masque in 1640 was the last play Davenant wrote for fifteen years. Those fifteen years were crowded with actions and dangers and responsibilities, and changes of place and interest, and occupations that left no time to write. He served six years in the King's army, spent three years with the Queen exiled at St. Germain, was knighted after the King's defeat at Marston Moore in 1644, where he was Colonel of Ordnance, again for two years was in France, and was appointed Royal Governor of Maryland but was captured before his ship was out of the Channel. He "lay in prison in extreme jeapordy," was released at the end of three years with a conditional pardon (in 1654, he "prayed to be freed from the constant surveillance by the Constable of the Tower"), and at length, about 1655, fairly secure, went to live in Rutland House in the City.

Davenant liked more than anything else to write plays and produce plays, his own or someone else's, and so, as he was living with some stability and could get the money, he set to work on an *Entertainment* which, as he put it, should "replenish a shrunken purse" and which should be given on a stage by actors yet should not bring down on it the Puritan veto.

What he wrote and published and staged at Rutland House in September, 1656, was "The First Day's Entertainment at Rutland House, by Declamation and Musick, after the manner of the Ancients." The Entertainment opened with "a flourish of musick" and a short Prologue—62 lines—in rhymed couplets. Next, as the stage directions of 1656 say, "A concert of instrumental music" sounded, "the curtains are suddenly opened, and in two gilded rostras appear, sitting, Diogenes, the cynic, Aristophanes, the poet, in habits agreeable to their country and professions." For 15 or 20 minutes, each declaimed, as the stage direction obscurely says, "against, and for, public entertainment, by moral representations." The audience was judge.

Diogenes spoke first, after "music adapted to [his] sullen disposition." He gave low worth to public assemblies, and music, and poetry. In *public assembly*—including plays—men showed at their worst, for wisdom never is spoken by the mingled breath of the crowd. *Music* is a deceitful art: it inflames and cheapens the feelings, and prevents that insight of the spirit and balance of mind which is wisdom. *Poetry*, too, deceives. "Like the pleasant vapors of Lesbian wine," it gives you "long dreams" in which you would roof your houses with tiles of gold and floor them with agate stones. Diogenes said this with no rancor, and with Davenant's wit and courteous irony. Instead of insisting, as most Roundheads did, only on evils, he granted that public entertainment with scenes and poetry and music gave pleasure. But the pleasure was weak and false and passing, and quite blunted man's moral growth. Now, ended Diogenes, "I shall retire to my tub."

Diogenes, Aristophanes said in response, had, like "your suburb-dog, ... all this while but barked at the Muses," the handmaids of Virtue. *Public assembly* had its uses. No man may carry out in private all necessary businesses. Wisdom is not always wisest when it is solitary. Meetings are part—a needed and virtuous part—of life. *Poets* have more wit than your cynic. Poets are "intentively employed in providing for the general happiness of human kind." Poets are "the busy secretaries of nature." Poetry makes wisdom understood and "even the severities of wisdom pleasant." Yet they had just seen Diogenes "busily bite and worry Poetry." *Music* brings concord to the discordant mind; it makes a man recognize what is good and gives him the "sudden strength to resist ... evils," it rouses the young to right ambitions and awakens "in the aged where hope is fallen asleep ..., the vital heat of the mind." Public opera with music, scenes, and poetry— those "several beauties [which] make up the shape of the opera" —is the "safest and surest way to understanding, for by it we see what we should otherwise never see," and we "gain from it experience which otherwise we should have been without." "But, excellent Athenians!" said Aristophanes at the end, "it were an unpardonable want of judgement in me to tire you with defending that which you already know needs no defense." Then "the curtains are suddenly closed, and the Company entertained by instrumental and vocal music," and a song which crowned the poet and sent the cynic back to "his old tub [and] his lanthron and his thridbare cloak."

Next came the second half in front of the curtain, more "instrumental music, after the French composition, [was] heard a while." Then the curtains parted and showed a man of Paris sitting in one gilded rostrum and a man of London in the other. First, the Parisian, speaking, by one account, in broken English (usually good fun in the theatre), extolled Paris. Next the Londoner spoke, "After a concert of Music, imitating the Waits of London," he claimed the pre-eminence of London (a sure patriotic hit): and he, of course, came off best. (Pepys, one night eight years after, read these speeches to his wife "in great mirth." The speeches read very well today.) Neither of the actors in the Second Half spoke about plays, poetry, or music. The curtains closed, again came instrumental music and a song crowning London, then an Epilogue, and with "a flourish of loud music" the end. A contemporary account, among *State Papers* Domestic, says that at the end were songs relating to the Victor [the Protector]; they are not in the printed text.

The Entertainment was given in a long narrow hall of Rutland House, which held perhaps four hundred people. It lasted one hour and a half, and the admission is said to have been a shilling. The stage was small: about 18 feet wide, 9 feet high, 18 feet deep. Staging was rich: the curtains were cloth of gold and purple, and the walls each side of the stage had the same hangings. The music, Davenant wrote in a preface, "was composed . . . by the most transcendent in England in that art." It was "recitative and therefore unpractic'd here." The composers were Charles Coleman (Doctor of Music, Cambridge, a member of Charles I's personal band. At the Restoration "he was granted the office of viol in ordinary amongst the lutes and voices in the king's private music." He died in 1664); Captain Henry Cook (a Royalist officer, a teacher of music, probably the writer of the Coronation Music, and Master of the Children of the Chapel Royal); Henry Lawes (a friend of Milton, composer, gentleman of the Chapel Royal, publisher); and George Hudson. The singers were Captain Henry Cook, Edward Coleman, Mrs. Coleman, and some "inconsiderable voices." The three chief singers were, the same year, in *The Siege of Rhodes*. For Davenant, *The First Day's Entertainment* was a triumph.

130

Davenant deserved his triumph. He had written a good play, quite his own, alive and free, yet he had shaped it to the time and the hearers and to his own purpose. For *The Entertainment* did three different and difficult things. (1) It did not offend Commonwealth religion, or prejudice, or law. (2) It pleased those who saw or read it. (3) It carried what Davenant wanted it to: that is, it bore witness to his belief, and it helped him, a little at least, to find how much of the old theatre the Puritans would allow.

(1) *The Entertainment* escaped offending Commonwealth law, religion, and prejudice. It was not a play, for it had no plot, no dramatic action; rather, it was like a masque, or an old morality play, or a set tableau with speeches and music. It was "private," for it was given in Davenant's house, though it was open to the public at Davenant's price. It was not professional, yet it was far from amateur in the finish and perfection of its staging and acting and speeches and music. Its actors were embodied abstractions, their talk pointing toward a moral end, yet Davenant put *actors* on a *stage*, and though each actor sat unmoving in his gilded rostrum, his presence made the scene real and his voice carried the thrill and the assurance of living speech. So, too, scenery and music and poetry and speaking were there, though muted for Puritan acceptance. Davenant was talking in favor of public plays which should have poetry and music, yet he was careful not to praise the plays and playhouses of the past, and careful to praise the present— England and London and Cromwell. And, too, with the wisdom of this world, he secured for his play before he put it on, "the influence of several powerful friends," among them Bulstrode Whitelocke. A week or so before the play was given, Davenant sent Whitelock the text "hot from the Press," and wrote, "[I am] making your Lordship my supreme Judge, though I despair ... of ... you [as] a Spectator. I do not conceive the perusal of it worthy any part of your Lordship's leisure, unless your antient relaxation to the Muses make you not unwilling to give a little [welcome] to Poetry; though in so mean a dress as this." Indeed Davenant's play did not "wrong ... Religion, Government, Safety, and Modestie."

(2) Davenant pleased his audience in many ways. *The Entertainment* had rich furnishings and hangings, the best singers in London, and "a concert of instruments," and it was animated by contrasts—discussion and music, Greece and England, Paris and London, poetry and prose, a cynic and a humanist. He wrote with wit and sense and charm, as a cultured man of his time might think and talk. He discussed what was of interest to intelligent listeners,

131

the sort who came to *The Entertainment,* and his writing had the pull of patriotism and the lift of poetry. He was never pedantic or proclaiming doctrine or straining to be profound. Davenant aimed to win his hearers to agreement not by argument but by the attraction which the mood of the play and his way of writing gave to what he said. All through the play was the poise of good manners, and the sparkle of fun, and a pleasant flattery to the hearers. They, he was saying, were the right judges; and with ready acceptance he left his play to them, sure that their verdict would be truer than his own judgment of the play, or his hope for it.

(3) *The Entertainment* said what Davenant wanted, and it did what he wanted it to. In it he bore witness that he believed some kinds of plays, even public plays, and some kinds of music and poetry, were good to have in Puritan England. And he found out, a little, what sort of public entertainment the Commonwealth would allow then or after a time. This inquiry was immensely important to Davenant; the theatre was his greatest interest, and writing and producing plays was his chief occupation. Whether the drama—not shadowy substitutes—could ever come back to the stage was a great question he was asking of the future. *The First Day's Entertainment* brought him part of his answer. Two years later the patriotic *Cruelty of the Spaniards in Peru*—more lavish in setting, more varied by dances and many actors, and more rich in costumes and sharply contrasted scenes, yet still almost a panorama with music and long speeches and "an acrobat"—gave him another part of his answer. And in 1658, with the fully dramatic *Siege of Rhodes* the answer was almost complete.

The Siege of Rhodes

Pepys liked Davenant's plays better than any others he read or saw, and of all Davenant's plays he liked best *The Siege of Rhodes.* It was given privately at Rutland House in 1656, just after *The First Day's Entertainment* ended its run of two weeks, a good run in Pepys's time. The first version had only one part, and took only one afternoon, and it did not have in it Roxalana, one of the chief characters. It was in verse, and was a series of situations given with music and recitative singing, not a centered quick-moving drama. Davenant kept rewriting *The Siege.* His second version was given at a public theater, the Cockpit Drury Lane, "in the winter of 1658 or early the next year." This version had two parts, each played on alternate afternoons; it added a fourth main character, and it had action and plot; its characters were not abstractions; its themes were love, war, jealousy, nobility of mind and action in men and women. It, clearly, was a drama. This version crowded the Cockpit, yet in spite of its popularity the party in power was so much "discontented" with it, and the House of Lords, which debated on the play, was "so against all stage-plays, and interludes and things of the like nature called opera" that it was suspended for a while; Davenant was arrested; and some playgoers were fined. But because during the last year of the Commonwealth the government was wholly attentive to confusion in public affairs, Davenant's play soon went on again, unhindered and unnoticed. The second year (1661) of Charles's return, *The Siege of Rhodes, Part One and Part Two* were staged the third time, at Lincoln's Inn Fields Theater. *Part One* opened Friday, June 28; Saturday, June 29, came *Part Two;* and through two weeks (Saturday, no performance) the two parts alternated day by day. Pepys saw *Part Two* on Tuesday, the second of July.

The Siege of Rhodes (Pepys, like Davenant, often called it the opera; Davenant even called it a poem) was a heroic romance written in verse and sung, for the most part, in recitative. It was given in 1661 by the Duke of York's Servants, of which Davenant was head. The plot is this: Solymon the Magnificent, great Sultan of Turkey, is besieging the Christian Knights of Malta, with whom are the young heroic Alphonso, a Sicilian duke, and his wife Ianthe, "The Silician flow'r." These two are devoted; yet when Ianthe goes to Solymon to plead for the city Alphonso grows jealous. So, too, does Roxalana, Solymon's beautiful and loved wife. Alphonso rushes out into the battle, is wounded, captured, taken to the headquarters of Solymon, meets Ianthe, repents his jealousy, is forgiven by Ianthe, and is set free by the magnanimity of Roxalana. Solymon, though he had vanquished Rhodes, is vanquished by the nobility of Ianthe and is lenient. At the end it is clear that Alphonso and Ianthe, Solymon and Roxalana, will live happily ever after. The interaction of these characters constitutes the play's romantic side. The rank of the characters, the war and rumors of war, the attacks and defenses of Rhodes, the voyages and returns, give it its high heroic tone.

* * * * * *

Pepys wrote four times in the Diary that he went to *The Siege of Rhodes, Part Two,* but never that he went to *Part One.* It is hardly credible that he did not see *Part One.* To find out from the Diary *alone* whether or not he did see it, has been an interesting try at puzzle-solving.

Probably he did see it. In the Diary, the props to probability are these: (1) Davenant was Pepys's favorite playwright and adapter and producer, and his company was under the patronage of the Duke of York, head of the Navy and Pepys's own patron, whom he much admired. Pepys saw at least twenty-five plays Davenant produced. (2) Of all Davenant's plays, Pepys liked best *The Siege*, "certainly (the more I read it the more I think so) the best poem that ever was wrote." He saw *Part Two* four times in a year and five months; he bought the printed text and read it to himself and to his wife and had it read to him; he talked of it in season and out, and sang its music and learned parts of its verse by heart. He seems to have been made happy by the play. (3) The two parts of *The Siege* make up one continuing story. (4) He knew *Part One* well, from reading it and talking with others and from hearing some of it sung by those who had sung in the first version of it. (5) The best song he wrote, *Beauty Retire*, sets to music eight lines of *Part Two*. Pepys was proud of the song; a picture of him in The National Portrait Gallery, painted when he was about thirty-three and once hanging in his house in Seething Lane, shows him holding the manuscript of it. (6) When the first and second versions of *The Siege* were first given, Pepys was desperately poor. He tells how scrupulously he and his wife, then just married—he at twenty-two, she at fifteen—had to economize. It may seem that he had no money then for play-going; yet he himself says he did go to a play of Davenant's before 1660.

In the Diary two entries go a little beyond probability and surmise. They are almost evidence that he did see *Part One* (almost evidence; not quite). (1) Pepys knew rather well two of the chief singers in the first version of the opera, Edward Coleman and Mrs. Coleman. One evening, October 31, 1665, at Pepys's house, they sang "part of the Opera." Pepys does not say *Part One* or *Part Two*. He does say that Mrs. Coleman did a "counterfeiting of Captain Cooke's part (Salymon), in his reproaching his man for cowardice, *Base Slave*." Nowhere in either part of *The Siege*, as the printed text gives it, does Solymon thunder *Base Slave* at anyone. He does, however, in Act II of *Part One* tell his "vizier"—"his man," as Pepys wrote—whom he holds responsible, that the Turkish Soldiers will be "fat slaves" if they turn coward. Pepys often quoted inaccurately.

Another entry in the Diary is part evidence that he went to *Part One*. On June 28, 1660, he wrote that he heard a man singing that

134

day whom he had heard sing "behind the curtaine formerly at Sir W. Davenant's opera." Davenant staged only four "operas" from 1655 to 1660—*The First Day's Entertainment, The Siege, Part One, The Cruelty of the Spaniards in Peru,* and *Sir Francis Drake.* Probably *The Entertainment* and *Sir Francis Drake* can be left from the list; if they can, the chance that Pepys saw *Part One* stands one to two.

Friday morning, September 23, 1664, Pepys got up late because he had been in great pain all night; "My cold and pain in my head increasing." He was sure that he got the cold "by flinging off my hat at dinner time [the noon before] and sitting with the wind in my neck." His wife had been unwell enough to have a maid "sit up by her all night." Through that morning he was busy and at noon, feeling ill, "dined with little heart." The afternoon brought more discomforts. When Pepys and other chief officers of the Admiralty were considering Naval affairs, the Comptroller of the Navy, Vice-Admiral Sir John Minnes, close to sixty-six, "took occasion, in the most childish and most unbeseeming manner, to reproach us all ... that he was not valued as Comptroller among us, nor did anything but only set his hand to paper, which is but too true; and every body had a palace, and he no house to lie." Pepys and the others listened, and seeing no good in answering, "all bore it." So, with the accumulations of the day he went home, and for pleasant readjustment he sat "late reading *The Siege of Rhodes* to my wife," and then he went to bed.

October first, the next year, Sunday, he and Captain Cooke and others went down the Thames in the yacht "Bezan" to the flagship, on which Admiral Lord Sandwich had summoned a council of war. That morning Pepys had been "Called up about 4 of the clock," had boarded the "Bezan," and "there finding all my company asleep" and "it beginning to be break of day," had stayed on deck awhile, and then had "slept a little." When they all were up, they "began to chat and talk and laugh, and mighty merry." They "spent most of the morning talking and reading of *The Siege of Rhodes.*" After the council of war, which began about two and lasted until late in the evening, Pepys had supper with the Admiral, went back on board the "Bezan," and "there to cards for a while and then to read again in *Rhodes* and so to sleep."

These two long quotations—there are others—suggest the satisfaction and the quick pleasure Pepys found in the play, and his habit of reading it and thinking and talking of it again and again in all sorts of moods and places and occupations.

CATHERINE OF BRAGANZA (1638-1705)

QUEEN OF ENGLAND (1662-1685)

When Pepys first saw Queen Catherine (September 7, 1662) she was twenty-four and had been married four months. She seemed to him young and innocent of life. Pepys found her "not very charming, yet she hath a good, modest, and innocent look, which is pleasing." ("Blessed be God!" Pepys wrote a month later, his wife continued in thrift and *innocence*." He liked the quality.) Charles II was thirty-two years old.

Whether or not the new Queen was good and beautiful and intelligent was important. She was much talked of everywhere. Before and after she came from Portugal, Pepys heard many opinions about her—from Lord Sandwich, who was the King's "Embassador in bringing over of the Queen"; from the Admiralty Treasurer and the Duke of York's Physician-in-Ordinary; and from others close about the King or the Queen. He heard, too, the common reports which were running through the Court and the town.

Pepys's Aunt Wight praised "the handsomeness of the Queen" to Pepys, who opposed his aunt "mightily, saying that if my nose be handsome, then is hers." Louis XIV (much for the marriage) assured Charles, his cousin, that "the infanta was a lady of great beauty and admirable endowments." He had once thought of marrying her. The Portuguese ambassador had earlier told the Chamberlain of the King "there was in Portugal a princess in beauty, person, and age very fit for him, and who would have a portion suitable to her birth and quality. She was indeed a Catholic, and would never depart from her religion; but she had none of that meddling activity that sometimes made persons of that faith troublesome . . .; she had been bred under a wise mother . . . she would be contented to enjoy her own religion, without concerning herself with what others professed." The Spanish Ambassador (violently against the marriage) said "she was deformed, had bad

136

health, and . . . would never have children." An English official in
Portugal reported to the Secretary of State: "The infanta is a lady
of incomparable virtue, of excellent parts, very beautiful. . . . We
shall be extremely happy in a Queen. She is as sweet a disposi-
tioned Princess as ever was born," intelligent, "but bred hugely
retired. She hath hardly been ten times out of the palace in her
life."

Lord Dartmouth, of the King's household, wrote that she was
"short and broad, and of a swarthy complexion; one of her fore-
teeth stood out, which held up her upper lip; and besides, she was
very proud and ill-favored." "A very little woman," wrote another
courtier, "with a tolerably pretty face." Lord Chesterfield, her
Chamberlain when she came to England, and thirty years old,
wrote: "You may credit her being a very extraordinary woman;
that is, extremely devout, extremely discreet . . . and the owner of
a good understanding. . . . She is exactly shaped, she has lovely
hands, excellent eyes . . . a pleasing voice ["a very low-voiced
lady," said Bishop Burnet of Salisbury], fine hair, and in a word,
is what an understanding man would wish a wife." John Evelyn,
the day he kissed her hand at Hampton Court, wrote in his Diary,
May 30, 1662. "The Queen arrived with a train of Portuguese ladies
in their monstrous fardingales . . . their complexions olivader [dark
olive] and sufficiently unagreeable. Her Majesty in the same habit,
her fore-top long and turned aside strangely. She was yet of the
handsomest countenance of all the rest, and, though low of stature,
prettily shaped, languishing and excellent eyes, her teeth wrong-
ing her mouth by sticking a little too far out; for the rest, lovely
enough." In England, she took at once to English dress. Admiral
Lord Sandwich wrote to Chancellor Clarendon: "she is a prince
of extraordinary goodness of disposition, very discreet and pious,
and there are the most hopes that ever were of her making the
King and us all happy." Lady Sandwich met Pepys just after she
had "come from Hampton Court . . . where the Queen hath used
her very civilly"; and, Pepys wrote, "My Lady tells me is a most
pretty woman, at which I am glad." The King's young sister, Henrietta Maria, Duchess of Orleans, "La belle Henriette," in 1670
wrote that "the Queen was a thoroughly good woman, not beautiful but virtuous and full of piety, and she commands the respect
of everyone."

Charles had never seen the princess before the day of their marriage at Portsmouth. He had seen a portrait said to be like her,
which has been described, somewhat intensely, as showing "a

lovely glowing brunette with enchanting eyes, and a rich profusion of chestnut hair" spread out and falling "each side of her face ... in parallel ... cannon curls [long tubular curls] to her waist." "One large tress," wrote Miss Strickland, "called a top-knot ... was combed slanting across the forehead." It was "a most extraordinary and unaccountable fashion," a fashion for royal Spanish ladies, but long outmoded even in Spain. Charles, after he had looked at the picture for a while, said "that person cannot be unhandsome."

The day after he had met the Queen at Portsmouth, Charles wrote to Chancellor Clarendon (May 21), "Her face is not so exact as to be called a beauty, though her eyes are excellent good, and nothing in her face that in the least degree can disgust one. On the contrary, she hath as much agreeableness in her looks as ever I saw, and if I have any skill in phisiognomy which I think I have she must be as good a woman as ever was born. Her conversation, as much as I can perceive, is very good, for she has wit enough and a most agreeable voice. You will wonder to see how well we are acquainted already; in a word, I think myself very happy, for I am confident our two humors will agree very well together."

That, as different persons of her day saw her, was the Lady whom Charles II married: young, frank, innocent, courageous; to Lord Sandwich, "all a recluse"; devout, protected, educated in a convent, and trained by her astute and affectionate Spanish mother in the duties and formality of the Court; a very great heiress ("the best match in her parish"); not beautiful, or if beautiful at all chiefly so because of her youth and animation and the goodness her face showed; speaking no English and so having to talk in Spanish with the King; kind, patriotic; guided by rectitude in action and thought.

Pepys heard many verdicts—direct verdicts from those close to the Queen and the echoed verdicts of others. The Diary of the next six years after 1662 shows more and more what verdict he thought was true.

—2—

The Queen had great pleasure in music and good taste in it and good training. In Portugal, music had been part of her usual day. The evening before she sailed from Lisbon to England on the "Royal Charles"—the ship was held in the harbor by lack of a breeze—her brother, the King (something of a musician, though a "frivolous, profligate and vicious young man," and later almost—

138

perhaps entirely—"an imbecile") and some nobles "embarked with their musical instruments in several barges, and coming under" the Queen's cabin windows, "sang carols, sonnets, madrigals and canzoni." Lord Sandwich's secretary told Pepys that on the voyage, though the Queen "never come upon the deck, nor put her head out of her cabin" [Portuguese court etiquette required the seclusion] yet she "did love my Lord's musique, and would send for it down to the state-room, and she [would] sit in her cabin within hearing of it" (May 24, 1662).

—3—

From the time it was suggested that Charles should marry her until his death, Catherine of Braganza was the aim of constant, powerful, varied attacks, some meanly spiteful (against her dancing, her dress, her liking tea and not wine, her complexion, and her character) and some great accusations (of plotting to poison the King and set fire to the City; of intriguing with the Pope, with the King of France; of innumerable lunacies under the moon). Her honor and life and freedom all were attacked, even by Parliament. In the air were schemes to divorce her; to put her in a convent; to kidnap her and ship her as a bond servant to some dim colony and forget her there; to have the King marry again without divorce.

In the attack were members of Parliament and of the Court; Lord Shaftsbury and others of the Opposition; political pamphleteers, hack satirists, among them Andrew Marvel; advocates of a republic; at least one bishop of the English church; the King's favorites, men and women; politician-patriots and professional apy-hunters; and such uncleanness as Titus Oates and his crew.

Pepys seems to have liked writing of the Queen, and the Diary reflects some of the warmth of his liking. To him she was far-away-the Queen, a lady he honored and admired. Her life was distant from his, and was obscured by distance and difference, and blurred to him by its brightness. That probably is why he never wrote of her with details, as he did of many others. Yet for him she never had the inhumanity of a news item. What he writes of her usually has the individuality this entry has: "The Queene is very well again; she speaks now very pretty English, and makes her sense out now and then with pretty phrases; as . . . meaning to say, she did not like such a horse so well as the rest, he being too prancing and full of tricks, she said he did make too much vanity."

—4—

The Diary has two pictures of the Queen at Whitehall. On the evening of November 15, 1666, Pepys, from the gallery, watched the Court ball given for the twenty-eighth birthday of the Queen. "Anon the house grew full, and the candles light [were lighted], and the King and Queene and all the ladies set [were in their places for the dance]. The King wore "rich silke and silver trimming, [and] the Duke of York and all the dancers were, some [in] cloth of silver, and others [in] other sorts, exceeding rich." The King took the Queen's hand and with fourteen other couples began to dance "the Bransles," [the brawl: a quick, rather merry, French dance; "a sort of cotillion, danced by a great number of persons"; "an old round dance, in which the performers join hands in a circle, and in which kissing the whole of the ladies, by each of the gentlemen in turn was one of the chief features." (Sir Frederick Bridge, *Samuel Pepys, Lover of Music*).] The King danced "rarely"—better than any other man. The ladies were "all most excellently dressed in rich petticoats and gowns, and dyamonds, and pearls . . . and it was, indeed, a glorious sight to see Mrs. Stewart in black and white lace, and her head and shoulders dressed in dyamonds, and the like a great many great ladies more, only the Queene none." The Queen was in mourning for her mother.

Two years after that, September 28, 1668, Pepys gave a second picture. He was "all the evening" at Whitehall "on the Queen's side; and it being a most summer-like day and a fine warm evening," some Italian singers came down the Thames "in a barge" singing. They stopped "under the leads [the terrace], before the Queen's drawing [room]"; and, because the music "was indeed very good together," with "one voice that did appear considerable," the voice of "Seignor Joanni" of the Queen's Chapel, "the Queen and ladies went out" on the leads "and heard them, for almost an hour."

Both these pictures were dim. They lack color and detail and centre yet they show that Pepys admired her. The two incidents deepen what else Pepys wrote about the Queen; and they suggest the reality of the life the Queen lived for twenty-three years in what Pepys called "a sad, vicious, negligent Court" (December 31, 1666).

—5—

Charles II died on February 6, 1685. While he lived, the Queen's childlessness made her the center of plots. At his death she became

140

of small importance. The energy of plotting turned upon King James. Catherine, after the revolution of 1688, could not live easily in England. When she went to Portugal in 1692, her going was hardly noticed except by those close around her, who knew her discretion and her kindness and her simplicity of goodness rising to wisdom. In Portugal she was greatly honored. She was twice regent for her brother, King Pedro II; and it is said she was one of the ablest rulers in Europe.

In 1700, when the Queen was sixty-two and Pepys was sixty-seven, he wrote to his nephew and heir John Jackson, who was making the Grand Tour and would soon be in Lisbon, a letter in which he speaks much in his old way of the Queen. She had been in Portugal about eight years then. Pepys was living at Clapham, with Will Hewer, and was not well.

"Clapham, October 8, 1700"

". . . . . . If this reaches you at Lisbon, I give you in charge to wait upon my Lady Tuke, one of the Ladies attending my once Royal Mistress, our Queen Dowager, there, a Lady for whom I bear great honor: nor, if she should offer you the honor of kissing the Queen's hand, would I have you to omit, if Lady Tuke thinks it proper, the presenting her Majesty, in most humble manner, with my profoundest duty, as becomes a most faithful subject."

PEPYS AT THE QUEEN'S CHAPEL

The Queen had her Chapel in the Palace of St. James's. Pepys did not go often to the Queen's Chapel. A chronicle of his goings and his opinion makes this calendar:

—1—

Queen Catherine first heard mass at her Chapel on Sunday, September 21, 1662, two weeks after she had come to London, "the first time it hath been ready for her." Pepys went to the mass. He "crowded" in "and there stood and saw the fine altar, ornaments, and the fryers in their habits, and priests . . . with their fine copes and many other very fine things." The noble form of the mass, the sonority of the Latin, though to Pepys strangely pronounced, the variety and power of the music, caught him into a new interest. Yet he did not feel at ease with the music: "I heard their musique, too; which may be good, but it did not appear so to me, neither as to their manner of singing, nor was it good concord to my ears." That was his first verdict. "The Queene very devout: but [he being Pepys] what pleased me best was to see my dear Lady Castlemaine. . . . By and by . . . a fryer with his cowl did rise up and preach a sermon in Portuguese; which I, not understanding, did go away."

In the next three and a half years he wrote little about the Queen's Chapel, and his comments are casual. Once (May 10th, 1663) he was "forced [at mass] in the crowd to kneel down"; on Ash Wednesday (February 24, 1664) he "staid and saw their masse, till a man came and bid me go out or kneel down"; and at another mass he "liked the musique."

The more he heard the music and the more he came to know it, the more he liked it. April 1, 1666, "a most pleasant warm day," wrote he did not so "dislike the musique"; two weeks later, Easter Day, 1666, he "heard . . . some of their musique, which is not so contemptible, I think, as our people would make it, it pleasing me very well; and, indeed, better than the anthem I heard afterward at White Hall." The "manner of doing" the sacrament was more "glorious" at the Queen's Chapel.

A year later (March 17, 1667) he heard the whole service and approved: "to the Queene's Chapel, and there heard a fryer preach with his cord about his middle, in Portuguese, something I could understand, showing that God did respect the meek and humble, as well as the high and rich. He was full of action, but very decent and good, I thought, and his manner of delivery very good."

The same year, 1667, at Easter, April 7, after sitting through a "lazy sermon" at Saint Olave's, he went to "the Italian musique at the Queen's chapel, whose composition is fine, but yet the voices of eunuchs I do not like ... nor am more pleased with it ... than with English voices [except that the Italians] do jump most excellently with themselves and their instruments." [He meant that Italian voice exactly suited Italian music.] "I am convinced more and more, that as every nation has a particular accent and tone in discourse, so as the tone of one not to agree with or please the other, no more can the fashion of singing to words, for that the better the words are set, the more they take in of the ordinary tone of the country whose language the song speaks, so that a song well composed by an Englishman must be better to an Englishman than it can be to a stranger, or than if set by a stranger in foreign words." The comment is judicious and quite to the point though tangled in expression. Pepy's taste and understanding in music were maturing.

Half a year later, Pepys went again. He liked the music "in itself pretty well as to the composition, but their voices are very harsh and rough that I thought it was some instrument that made them so" (September 8, 1667). Christmas Eve, 1667, Pepys went to the Chapel, his "design being to see the ceremony, this night being the eve of Christmas." For once, he did not go as a critic of music or of anything else. By energy he got up "almost to the [altar] rail, and with a great deal of patience stayed from nine at night to two in the morning, in a very great crowd.... The Queen was there, and some ladies. But, Lord! what an odde thing it was for me to be in a crowd of people, here a footman, there a beggar, here a fine lady, there a zealous poor papist, and here a Protestant, two or three together, come to see the show. I was afeard of my pocket being picked very much.... Their musique very good indeed, but their service I confess too frivolous ... there can be no

143

real zeal go along with it. . . . But all things rich and beautiful."
When the service was over he took his coach "which waited and
away through Covent Garden." At the Rose Tavern he drank some
burnt wine and then drove round the city, "it being a fine, light,
moonshine morning" (December 24, 25, 1667). He went to bed,
close to daylight, "and slept well, and rose about nine, and to
church, and there heard a dull sermon."

Easter Day of 1668, March 22, six years after his first going
there, he went "to the Queen's Chapel, and there did hear the
Italiana sing; and indeed their musique did appear most admirable to me, beyond anything of ours; I was never so well satisfied
in my life with it." This is quite another verdict from his first one.
Six months later (September 27, 1668) he heard more "good singing" at the Chapel.

—2—

A summary of what Pepys gained at the Queen's Chapel is in
part this:

He heard a kind of music new to him, quite different from the
usual music of England. The music at the Chapel, even the traditional Church music, was Italian, composed and sung or played
by Italians "very skilled in their art." The Queen seems to have
cared little for English music or even for French, much of which
was given in the King's Chapel Royal. She had favored Italian
music in Portugal. Under her patronage Italian opera was given in
London in January, 1674.

He heard music played and sung as well as it was anywhere else
in Europe. The Queen had many and most competent musicians.
The Master of the Queen's Music—a composer and singer—was an
Italian, and so were many of her other musicians, of whom she had,
in 1674, as part of her household, "12 musicians at 120 pounds
apiece" and eight "boys of the Chapel," who with her Master of
Music were paid "440 pounds a year."

The music at the Queen's Chapel probably was in itself the best
music Pepys heard. It was better in composition and substance; it
had variety, though it always was within the cannons of Church
music; and it was both more austere—more traditional, more tested
by time—than the music Pepys was used to, and fresher with the
new art and fervor of Italy. At first Pepys clearly did not like it at
all. He was not at home with it. Then as he heard it more often,
he found it increasingly noble in composition and tone, less personal, more elevated and lasting. At the King's Chapel the music

might interest him partly because one friend of his had composed it, or another sang or played it, or because for the first time he heard a new kind of organ or a choir of twenty-four violins or seventeen trumpets with kettledrums, or what not. At the Queen's Chapel he heard music which was impersonal, detached from any interest outside the music itself. That quality had made him not greatly care at first for the music.

At any rate, what he heard educated him in music. It made him listen more absolutely and think more deeply about what he heard. It got him to require, and to expect, the best. The Diary ends May 1, 1669. Six weeks before it ended, Pepys went to the Queen's Chapel on another Easter (April 11); and he wrote: "Excellent musick, but not so good as by accident I did hear there yesterday, as I went through the Park." Pepys, it seems, took for granted that music at the Queen's Chapel always would be good. The music there set a standard for the other music he heard.

—3—

Easter Sunday, 1669, Pepys took his wife to the Queen's Chapel, "the first time I ever did it." He sets down the facts without explaining. Perhaps his waiting six years does not need explanation. Perhaps entries in the Diary suggest one.

March 28, 1664, when he went home Monday afternoon his wife told him that "Father Fogourdy hath been with her to-day, and she is mightily for our going to hear a famous Reulé preach at the French Embassador's house: I pray God he do not tempt her in any matters of religion, which troubles me." "Father Fogourdy," Pepys had written was "an Irish priest, of my wife's and her mother's acquaintance in France, a sober discreet person, but one that I would not have converse with my wife for fear of meddling with her religion, but I liked the man well" (February 6, 1664). Elizabeth Pepys was the daughter of a Frenchman, Alexandre le Marchant de St. Michel, turned Huguenot when he was twenty-one.

Another entry four years after the first is (October 25, 1668) "my wife did find me embracing the girl [their maid Deb] ... which occasioned the greatest sorrow to me that ever I knew in this world." His wife was struck mute and grew angry, and so her voice come to her." Pepys found that he had little to say. He went "to bed, and my wife said little also, ..., but about two in the morning waked me and cried, and fell to tell me as a great secret that she was a Roman Catholique and had received the Holy Sacrament, which troubled me."

Pepys did not tell, straight out, why he never had taken his wife to the Queen's Chapel. The entries may suggest a reason; they may not. To most churches, except to the morning service at St. Olave's, Pepys seems to have gone by himself.

He may have liked to go alone to the Queen's Chapel. Or he may have had a reason—a fear of its Catholic influence—for waiting six years before he took his wife there with him. Or he may not have had a reason at all.

"MY GREAT LETTER OF REPROOF"

Pepys first heard of Lord Sandwich's infatuation with Mrs. Betty Becke, "a woman of a very bad fame and very imprudent," in early August, 1663, the tenth. (*Mrs., Mistress*, might or might not stand for marriage; Pepys writes "Mrs. Margaret Pen" when Peg Pen was nine). Within a week he did "resolve to speak to him of it if I can seasonably" (August 17). Then he decided he had best write, and November 18, he wrote. It was a difficult letter. He had to tell Lord Sandwich that common report said he was making a fool of himself, and openly: and that he was "being debauched. Equally he had to show that though he, Pepys, might seem impertinent and presumptuous and ungrateful, he was none of these. Always, with humble gratitude he kept in mind the kindnesses of Lord Sandwich to him. "[E]very bit of bread I eat tells me I owe [all] to your Lordship (November 18, 1663).

The letter was right in its substance and its tone. It was definite in facts, showed full confidence in Lord Sandwich, and made clear the dangers in such public gossip. Under all Pepys tells, his honesty of purpose shows, and his respect for Lord Sandwich and for himself.

The letter is characteristic of Pepys's moral view. It never touched the abstract right or wrong of Lord Sandwich's conduct. Pepys was concerned that loud gossip at Court and in the City was saying Lord Sandwich was bringing scandal "upon himself" and was "expos[ing] the safety of [his] honour"; he was negligent of his duties in the Navy; he had raised "a general coldness in all persons towards" himself; his way of life "occasion [ed] . . . scandal to your Lordship," and was a "gratifying of some enemies" and "the wounding of more friends [than Pepys was] able to tell." In short, Lord Sandwich's conduct falsified his real qualities, laid him open to ridicule, and endangered his career, and his favor with the King. Only Lord Sandwich himself could dissipate the dangers.

Characteristically, Pepys did not argue his points. And, characteristically, he did not suggest to Lord Sandwich that he do this or that. The letter said plainly that scandal was out against him and what the scandal was. Having told this, Pepys repeated that he wrote the letter with all "dutifull intents," and then "in all himility [he took his] leave," being always "Your Lordship's most obedient Servant, S. P." This was the letter he sent November 18.

The letter was not written in a flash of decision, on impulse. After he heard the gossip, in August, he weighed whether or not he had best tell Lord Sandwich anything. When he had settled that question, he spent time deciding whether he should talk to Lord Sandwich or write, and picking out what he should tell. Sunday afternoon, November 15, Pepys in his office "drew up a letter to my Lord, stating to him what the world talks concerning him, and leaving [action] to him and myself to be thought of by him as he pleases, but I have done but my duty in it." Two days later he read the letter to Mr. Moore, a relative of Lord Sandwich's and an old friend of his own, to get "his advice about sending it." Mr. Moore assured him the letter was admirable, should be sent, and offered to copy it and send it "as from . . . his hand." That Pepys would not allow. He was "unwilling [the letter] should come from anybody but myself." Late that afternoon, when Mr. Moore had gone, Pepys "did take a copy of it to keep by me in shorthand and sealed them [the letter and a fifty-word enclosing note] up to send tomorrow by my Will" (November 17, Tuesday). Wednesday morning he sent the letter by Will Hewer, "who did give it into his [Lord Sandwich's] owne hand." Part of the entry for that day, a busy day for Pepys, is: "I pray God give a blessing to it, but confess I am afeard what the consequence may be to me of good or bad, which is according to the ingenuity [open mind] that he do receive it with. However, I am satisfied that it will do him good, and that he needs it."

Pepys comes out well in this. To write Lord Sandwich was an act of courage, for he knew he might lose the help of Lord Sandwich and lower his own future. Without the backing of Lord Sandwich he would get on slowly, if at all. However much he had gained in the first three years as Clerk he still had far to travel; and he was ambitious, intensely so. Writing the letter was like other acts of his by which he put in hazard his life or his career. He had stayed in London through the Great Plague, though he felt the solemnity of the time wherein "a man cannot depend upon living two days." He had sent his wife to Woolwich when the

148

Plague had come into the City, and had put his "things and estate in order, in case it should please God to call me away, which God dispose of to his glory!" And he had made a will and prepared himself for death both, he hoped, "as to soul and body." Then he went on with his work, which was heavy because the heightened Dutch War was fought almost wholly at sea.

It is startling that Pepys ever considered writing a reproof. Next to his wife, Lord Sandwich was the person about whom his life centered. He had always felt honored that he stood well with one so highly placed and so deserving of that place. He was grateful for the continuing good opinion of Lord Sandwich and for his help, which began even before the days at St. Paul's School.

Pepys's liking and admiration and gratitude did not fade him to an echo. He did not always think that Lord Sandwich took the right action or made the best decision. He held his own views, often in opposition, about government and religion and education and management of many Naval matters, and he made his own choices in books and plays and music and people. Pepys never intruded. If Lord Sandwich asked his opinion he gave it, and having given it did not persist. Nowhere else in the Diary did Pepys ever tell Lord Sandwich that a serious decision of his or an intended action had best not be carried out. He was devoted to Lord and Lady Sandwich, who had been kind to him and his wife since the early meagre days. He had affection for their children, to whom he had once for a time been half tutor, half trusted servant, and whom he still often served.

Through the Diary, from the first page, Lord Sandwich moves as Pepys saw him: with august authority, dignified, held rather in awe; mature though only eight years older than Pepys; aloof yet always his kind patron and the head of the family and its protector; an Earl, at twenty colonel in the Commonwealth army, and then General at Sea [Admiral], ambassador to Spain, special envoy to bring the new Queen home to England, Deputy Chancellor, Vice-Admiral of England, a splendid figure at Court, Knight of the Garter; the embodiment of an eminence and stability and strength which was somehow like that of England's. Yet Pepys knew most of the good and bad Lord Sandwich did or left undone, and the varying levels of his motives and morals. Pepys knew that Lord Sandwich was imperfect, sometimes in very hot water, indeed; that he was, after all, part of common mankind, who, as the Prayer Book reminded, all like sheep have gone astray. Pepys accepted that even the highest and most honored were fallible.

149

One day, after "hearing him [the King] and the Duke [of Monmouth] talk, and seeing and observing their manner of discourse," Pepys wrote, "And God forgive me! though I admire them with all the duty possible, yet the more a man considers and observes them, the less he finds of difference between them and other men, though (blessed be God!) they are both princes of great nobleness and spirits" (July 26, 1665).

What Lord Sandwich had violated, it seemed to Pepys, was his duty—to his family, his friends, his position as admiral and gentleman, his own dignity and self-respect. Pepys believed that he himself and other men had a duty to their family, their friends, their work, their class, their country—and to themselves. To betray such duties openly, for "private pleasure," was as much an act of treason as to betray a public duty for money. A man's moral business was to find and to accept some written and unwritten laws of behaviour, to keep them if he could, to be sorry when he broke them, and to try again; and, though he broke them often, never to show public disrespect for them. Pepys, it seems, held that the written laws, because they were more obvious and more limited, were easier to know and to follow, though difficult enough; but that the unwritten laws, because they were inherent and so touched men's behaviour deeply, were more important and more complex, and harder to obey. They were like the common law in government. To know the unwritten laws required an understanding of civilized traditions and actions and an alertness to duty. To uphold them was the special responsibility of men of intelligence and high position.

It is easy to impute mean motives for writing the letter. It is easy enough to say Pepys wrote from self-interest, since he knew if Lord Sandwich went down, he would go, too; besides Lord Sandwich owed him 700 pounds. Or it can be said Pepys felt satisfaction in telling Lord Sandwich what he ought not to do, in getting back at him; in, for once, reversing their usual position of inequality. Or Pepys himself may have turned gossip, wholly a busybody, mixing into what was no concern of his. Or he was a hypocrite; he affected to be upset by Lord Sandwich's affair while he and others (unwritten to) carried on the same kind of intrigue. Or he was a fool for a dunce-cap, too dull to know the lack of propriety in his intrusion.

To see the letter written from such motives, is to see Pepys as fussy, talkative, pushing, peering, light-minded, unthinking; rather likable, rather vulgar, rather foolish; as caring much for money though ready to spend it in show; as a strange little man, whose language ("So to bed") and food and medicines and music and feeling and wife and spelling and opinions and clothes and alternate vows and lapses, are all childish and more than half silly; and whose Diary, though amusing, of course, unfailingly refreshes the reader's (and today's) superiority. To find such motives for writing the letter, is to miss the whole quality of the Diary—and of Pepys.

The letter should be read as a whole. After all, it is not the elements in the letter—the facts, the phrasing, the piloting of its substance from the first word to the signature—that are the letter. They are the parts of it; they make it up. The letter is a whole and should be read as a whole. Read so, it shows why Pepys wrote Lord Sandwich. The effect it leaves on anyone's mind and spirit is likely to fix his opinion of Pepys.

The letter is clear and direct and sincere and dignified and restrained. Pepys wrote such a letter because he forgot himself in writing it. He is out of the letter because he was sure that what he was writing was important and he was not. The letter is from one quite in earnest, quite certain of what he has to say and of its seriousness. Diffused but clear all through the letter, Pepys's loyalty to Lord Sandwich shows, and his pride in him, and his liking and respect, and his anxiety over the open and unseemly display, and his care for Lord Sandwich's position and honor. The letter shows the practical good sense (too worldly, perhaps) on which Pepys based his action; his liking for clear-cut examination and definite remedy, for exact definition; and it shows what may fairly be called his humility. These qualities make up the air, the solvent, which holds what Pepys says to Lord Sandwich. The letter as a whole is good proof of what Pepys was "as of November 1663."

Pepys had great anxiety after he sent the letter (Wednesday, the eighteenth). The next day, with relief, he heard that it had "wrought well upon" Lord Sandwich. Friday, he went to Lord Sandwich's but Lord Sandwich was not at home. Early on Sunday he went again and he and Lord Sandwich talked a long time, both rather awkward and self-conscious. Lord Sandwich thanked Pepys for his "tenderness and good will"; he did "assert the civility of the ... young gentlewoman, for whose reproach he was sorry"; and then, after more talk of the letter, he became silent. Pepys, at the end, was in tears. He was so troubled that he could not "remember three words" of the two sermons he heard that day. It was a comfort to tell his wife "what had passed," and, though a much less one, to work at his office, "doing business only to keep

[his] mind employed till late." So Pepys felt, continuously, the first days and weeks.

Lord Sandwich's "foreigness," with ups and downs half-imagined by Pepys and fully written of, went on the rest of the year. Yet time lessened the tensions. Pepys did not write so much about Lord Sandwich. Lord Sandwich lent his coach and six to Pepys for the funeral of Pepys's cousin Edward; and in most was often as he had been, even if at times he showed some coldness. At any rate, Pepys knew that after the letter Lord Sandwich "wholly left Chelsy, and the slut, and . . . he do follow his business, and becomes in better repute than before" (December 14, 1663).

Even at the end of January their relations were uneasy, not quite the old ways. It was inevitable, Pepys thought, that Lord Sandwich "do look upon me as a remembrancer of his former vanity, and an espy upon his present practices." But as time went by they thought less about the strange episode of the letter, and, though slashes of memory cut at each of them now and then, the estrangement faded out and the old relation came again and increased.

MORALITY

Though the Diary shows the influence of the Bible and the Book of Common Prayer, Pepys, like many of his time and his class, never thought of the Church as a spiritual guide. The Established Church was important in the social and political structure of England, and his parish church was a needed part of his own way of living. He went on Sundays to St. Olave's Hart Street, personally and officially his church. He upheld the Anglican Establishment and its code and its embodiments. He felt deep respect, if small emotion, for that religion inherited and maintained by law in England; and, besides, he found pleasure in a beautiful church building and good church music—Catholic or Protestant—and in the ritual.

The Diary has no conscious concern even for a sentence with the life of the spirit which is in men. In spiritual speculations and spiritual struggle Pepys shows no interests. Yet at bottom he was a moralist. He had rules and he wanted to act by conscience, and he was interested in people and concerned about them, and many of them he sympathized with and understood, inside his limitations. Of sins of the flesh and of the mind, as long as they did no injury and were not signs of decay or of a mean or pinched or blunted nature, he was tolerant—even of his own. To be sure, he regretted his own and wanted to overcome them, but perhaps unconsciously he took them as inevitable parts of living.

The place of morality was chiefly in personal relations. He made morality as he saw morality one test of his aims and acts at home, in his business, and toward his friends, though he never called it by so abstract a name. He was not at all certain that the morality he followed could be equally active in large relations. At any rate, it was more active and more binding and more likely to be kept in intimate individual relations than it was in the wide sweep of social complexity. Though in his personal life he tried—and then tried again—to find and to follow what was morally right or at least decent, he did not agonize over his failures. Being a moralist, he was sorry and often sharply blamed himself, but he got back his equanimity fairly soon.

In the Diary he blames himself for having done a special action, not for having broken a general law. He seldom, almost never, writes of large, underlying, directing principles; he neither named nor seems to have been concerned with such abstractions. Certainly, his repenting a specific lapse does imply he accepted a law as the test for his actions, but he was instinctively specific; he wrote and thought and felt concretely. He was no moral philosopher. His opinions and his purposes passed directly into acts; and so it seems only fair to think less of his sense of law than of the moral quality in his actions.

* * * * * *

Morality had no part in the judgment Pepys gives of plays or sermons or music. A play was "the most insipid ridiculous play I ever saw in my life"; it was "an indifferent good play," "acted to my great content," "ill acted," "a very merry and pretty play," "too sad and melancholy"; and not uncommonly he added a comment like this one: "My pleasure was great to see ... so many great beauties" in the audience. He appreciates saintness in a man; he yet almost never notices its presence or absence in a sermon. A sermon made him "angry," or it was "dry," "well spoken," "much matter well put," "tedious," "freshly spoken," "a dull drowsy one," silly or ridiculous or "pragmatic," and more than one he "slept through." He remembered a sermon because "here preached a confident young coxcomb," or because of some unusual fact which had nothing to do with the sermon. He tells for instance that he went to "the French church at the Savoy ... a pretty place it is ... and, which I never saw before, the minister do preach with his hat off." Music, he often felt intensely but even when he felt it intensely it gave him not much beyond a flooding sense of delight. He never suggests any relation between morality and music. Nothing he wrote in the Diary implies that music could "raise and sustain" the spirit, or that he ever imagined it might.

It is typical of Pepys moral view that when Lord Sandwich was entangled, Pepys jeopardized his standing by his letter to Lord Sandwich; and it is just as typical that he did so because the infatuation with Mrs. Betty Becke threatened Lord Sandwich's reputation and position.

154

Pepys kept his lapses in impulse and action private, shut from public sight. He never, as Lord Sandwich did in 1663, put them on display. A few—the King and a half dozen besides—might violate the code of public discretion, though even they not without sharp comment; to others, gross violation brought a negative social verdict and the swift penalty of exclusion. This Pepys knew, but knowledge of it was not needed to keep him from publishing himself.

One reason he submerged his lapses was that he thought them wrong. To show them was to do harm. He believed society had moral structure which should be preserved, moral laws by which he was bound and under which he ought to live. And in spite of his repeated defections he honored law. He did not see clearly what the laws were or what inspired them, and some laws which he upheld may be small and earthy and his choice a moral mistake, but that he upheld what he thought was right makes clear he had beliefs and put them in action. Many rules he honored and carried out in talk and work were true enough to satisfy the most demanding moralist. As the Diary shows, he stood up well during the Plague and the Great Fire, and toward his kin, and under attempts to bribe him, and in all his work as Clerk of the Acts; and he wished, and tried, to stand up well in his relations with his wife. After the Diary was ended, he met steadily the death of his wife, recurring illness, fear of going blind, political defeat, imprisonment, accusations of apostasy and treason and dishonesty, and the finality of age.

Another reason Pepys kept his lapses to himself and to shorthand was that he thought them slight matters, in the long run not important. They harmed no one, he thought, or at the worst only a little. He picked them up casually (though under strong impulse) and as casually put them down; not without shame at the end, for they violated his moral rules and lowered the temperature of his self esteem, and sometimes they brought unhappiness to another person. Yet he felt (and was) in control of his triflings. They would never be the main forces in his life.

As the Diary shows he did not let them touch, much less affect, what was essential: his affection for his wife, his family loyalty, his work, his building the Navy, his social standing, his friendships, his music, his itch to follow fresh inquiries, his large purpose to deal justly with all men. These and matters like them were serious matters, to be kept in another world from private dallyings. They were the real thing, the meaning of what he did, the certainty, the core of it. They were inviolate.

* * * * * *

Pepys pretty much felt that an act of his was good if it brought material comfort to his body or mind. He once wrote in the Diary: "So home and to dinner, where I confess, reflecting upon the ease and plenty that I live in, of money, goods, servants, honour, every thing, I could not but with hearty thanks to Almighty God ejaculate [impulsively make a short prayer] my thanks to him while I was at dinner, to myself" (June 23, 1666). The sentence shows, too, that, he had read the Bible and Shakespeare and had caught some of their colors if he had not felt their depth.

He did and thought some evil things. Physical immoralities were a fashion of the time, common enough around him. They were a part of his life; but they were not all of it, nor the greater part. How great a part they were is easily distorted. And Pepys, in spite of the company he had with him when he did wrong, felt he was doing wrong, and he made vows which he wrote out and seriously re-read. At almost the end of Diary is the entry: "I do find that it is much the best for my soul and body to live pleasing to God and my poor wife, and will ease me of much care as well as much expense" (November 20, 1668). The sentence does not show in it a mind morally sensitive; the ending is all wrong. In his vows, as in his music, Pepys did not touch the truths of the spirit. He was not capable, it seems, of the deep reality of repentance.

ONE VALUE OF THE DIARY
TO PEPYS

Pepys had no instinct for discipline. He did not naturally find a standard for his living, test by it, accept the decision of the test, and live by the decision. Neither his temperament nor his training gave him that balance. Pepys had strong blood.

Very early, however, his intelligence began to make him sure that discipline must be the guiding power for him if ever he was to get ahead. Discipline was living right. Discipline was another name of success. Sunlight and dancing impulse often were more attractive than sobriety; yet at St. Paul's School, where he went from ten to seventeen, and at Cambridge, after he was seventeen, success was his serious business, and he did not let any shimmering gay wilfulness spoil it.

Pepys very early learned that success—discipline—took a cool, practical mind and a strong will. It required looking down opposite roads before deciding on one of them and then taking the road which gave the most practical gain in route or at the end. Pepys was never likely to start running, as Christian had, toward a Celestial City of hoped-for and infinite reward but of no seen and measurable and worldly gain.

Pepys, the Diary shows from the first, kept discipline in the public and private matters he thought important. It is well to remember that he was sure discipline was morally right. His eyes and his will were on doing right in his Admiralty work, which was new and serious; on getting ahead in position and money; on his relations with Lord Sandwich; and, most important and difficult, on his life with Elizabeth Pepys, though in that he found his discipline hardest to follow. To his wife he was at times unreasonable and quite wrong. He contradicted his love for her by his actions and talk. Yet as a whole he held to discretion. He knew when and where he dared explode temperamentally; he seldom against his will let discipline slip in public.

Alone, quite free, among his publically silenced impulses and daydreams and disturbing desires and irritations and prejudices, quite alone, he went the ways of the wind. He had thoughts and mental pictures and did acts—though not openly—which had no agreement with the conduct he had decided to follow. Judged by common rule, Pepys in private did make a fool of himself. Few of these transgressions got into open actions. Usually the lapses were within the secrecy of his mind—moods, sharp opinions, desires, imaginings he knew he never could show out in public display.

By writing them in the Diary in a shorthand cipher he got great relief, and great pleasure. The Diary was the only place—the Diary was a *place*, a true world to him—where he could follow the flow of one part of his nature. The recording of that unacted life had value for him. It let him live in the experience of words (very real to a nature like his) what he could not live in the open. To live so, was safe. Since no one else was to read what he had written, no one was astonished, and he himself did not stay balked and dumb, and he had the satisfaction of keeping the moral road he was determined to follow in public. His vagaries of feeling and opinion which went into the Diary did not harm anyone. So he thought.

Pepys was surprisingly hard-headed and strong-willed in following what to him was the main chance. He became more and more able to subdue into silence and shorthand an impulse he enjoyed but disapproved of, and more able to recognize and so dominate "the natural aptness I have to be troubled at anything that crosses me" (February 7, 1662).

More and more what he did and said in public had the qualities proper for public display to other people. He liked being, and being thought, a main-chance conservative, business-like official and yet an artistic and scholarly, companionable, alert, upper-class gentleman. Before the Diary ended he had his public recognition. He was Fellow of the Royal Society, Younger Brother of Trinity House, honorary burgess of Portsmouth, Justice of the Peace, Master of Arts from Cambridge, Commissioner for the Affairs of Tangier, deputy for the Clerk of the Privy Seal, Member of the Clothworker's Guild, Assistant in the Corporation of Royal Fishery, governing member of St. Olave's; and he had had his portrait painted twice, and a miniature and a bust made of himself. As the Diary ended, he was soon to become an elder in St. Olave's and to stand for Parliament.

Pepys enjoyed those public attentions; yet in the Diary he found release from publicity.

In the Diary he could sow wild oats unseen and, he was certain, with no harm. Though he probably never thought about it, he had found a discreet resultant of the two opposing forces in his nature, a balance. Near the end of the 1660's, the rule of law which he had established for himself and had earlier held to with difficulty, tempered into habit. That is, it almost tempered; for wayward thoughts and moods—less often action—would at times again flash violent colors across his sky.

So, tenaciously, year after year, as the Diary tells, he built up the Navy, made friends, showed his genius in business, bettered his standing, saved money, kept at his music, learned an immense range of things he felt he should know (ship designing and timber and cordage, for instance, and the multiplication table and accounting, Tangier, some chemistry and physics, Italian and Spanish and French), and enjoyed things which, like his music, were purely pleasure. He showed openly his genuine, fresh, wide, abundant, earnest, endless interest; his delight in what was around him for serious use or for the minute. And during the ten years, for matters not suited to public light he had his Diary.

TWO DINNERS

Pepys liked people and the amenities of life—wit, good manners, good conversation, elegance. He liked to talk and he liked to listen and he did both well, for he was intelligent and sensitive and charming. He was a social person. And he "did enjoy mightily to have friends at [his] table."

Pepys wrote of two dinners he gave. The first dinner was in the first month of the Diary, when he lived in Axe Yard. The second was in the last year of the Diary, nine years after the first.

I

January 26, 1660: "Home from my office to my Lord's lodgings where my wife had got ready a very fine dinner—viz. a dish of marrow bones; a leg of mutton; a loin of veal; a dish of fowl, three pullets, and two dozen of larks all in a dish; a great tart, a neat's tongue, a dish of anchovies; a dish of prawns and cheese," and wine. His company was his gentle, withdrawn father and his querulous mother, both about sixty; dull Thomas Fenner, his uncle the blacksmith, and his ailing wife; Kate, Uncle Fenner's daughter, and her husband, Anthony Joyce (He kept The Three Stags tavern. "Lord!" Pepys wrote six years later, "how sick I am of [his] company, only hope I shall have no more of it a good while"); Mary, her sister, and her husband, Will Joyce, Anthony's brother, a "silly prating fellow," "a talkative coxcombe"; Pepys's brother Tom, whose part seems to have been a silent one, with attention to the wine; Doctor James Pierce, surgeon to the Duke of York, whom Pepys liked, and his wife, whom Pepys (but not Mrs. Pepys) thought "a beauty." The Joyce brothers were ill-mannered, smartly conceited, incessant and satisfied talkers (Will, the more so), and given to quarrels and drinking. Pepys stood by them as kin and avoided them as persons. At the dinner, Mrs. Pierce appeared "so gallant that it put the two women quite out of courage"; "W. Joyce talking after the old rate and drinking hard, vexed his father and mother and wife"; and the Pierces were well-mannered but astonished at the assortment of guests. "We were as merry as I could frame myself to be in the company." When, after dark, they all went away, "I and my wife were much pleased."

II

(January 22, 1669) That afternoon Pepys was at his "office to dispatch a little business, and then home to look after things against to-morrow, and among other things was mightily pleased with the fellow that come to lay the cloth, and fold the napkins, which I like so well, as that I am resolved to give him 40s. to teach my wife to do it. So to supper, with much kindness between me and my wife, which, now-a-days, is all my care, and so to bed." The next morning, "Up, and again to look after the setting things right against dinner, which I did to very good content." After being in his office until noon he went home, "and there I found my Lord Sandwich ["who had never yet eat a bit of bread in my house"], Lord Peterborough [who had been the first Governor of Tangier], and Sir Charles Harbord." Sir Charles was twenty-nine, an officer in the Navy, knighted four years earlier, and nominated five days before my Lord Sandwich as paymaster at Tangier. He was a young, devoted friend of Lord Sandwich fifteen years or so younger; and he died with him on the "Royal James," fighting the Dutch, off the Suffolk coast, in 1672. Soon, to the dinner "comes my Lord Hinchingbroke [Lord Sandwich's eldest son], Mr. Sidney [Montagu, Lord Sandwich's second son], and Sir William Godolphin [M.P., powerful at Court, Ambassador to Spain in 1671]. And after greeting them, and some time spent in talk, dinner [prepared, it seems, by a man cook] was brought up, one dish after another, but a dish at a time, but all so good; but, about all things, the variety of wines, and excellent of their kind, and all in so good order, that they were mightily pleased, and myself full of content at it: and indeed it was, of a dinner of about six or eight [main] dishes, as noble as any man need to have, I think; at least, all was done in the noblest manner that ever I had any, and I have rarely seen in my life better anywhere else, even at the Court. After dinner, my Lords to cards, and the rest of us sitting about them talking, and looking on my books and pictures, and my wife's drawings, which they commend mightily; and mighty merry all day long, with exceeding great content, and so till seven at night; and so took their leaves, it being dark and foul weather. Thus was this entertainment over, the best of its kind, and the fullest of honour and content to me, that ever I had in my life: and shall not easily have so good again." The dinner so delighted Pepys he could not stop writing of it or write coherently. Food, guests, talk, all were perfect. After the noble dinner came a seventeenth century contrast: "So to my wife's chamber, and there supped, and got her Cut my hair and look my shirt, for I have itched mightily these 6 or 7 days, and when all comes to all she finds that I am lousy; having found in my head and body about twenty lice, little and great, which I wonder at, being more than I have had I believe these 20 years."

The two dinners show much of what Pepys wanted in life, and they measure the distance he went in nine years toward living the way he wanted to. Each shows his intense, inherent satisfaction in propriety and wit, good talk light or serious, good manners, elegance, and in having a thing done right, even the folding of a napkin. The two show that back in 1660 Pepys still valued what he had valued in 1669.

PEPYS AND ELIZABETH PEPYS

The part Elizabeth Pepys had in the life of Pepys is hard to get into a focus of truth. What he wrote about her seems contradictory and complex. Yet complex as it is, it has unity. The bewildering succession of moods simplifies into his pride and love and need of her; his feeling of responsibility for her; his sympathy for her; and at times his helplessness and incomprehension.

Division

Pepys obscured this unity in one way by telling so many of his foolish and primitive actions—pulling "her by the nose" (April 5, 1664); striking her and kicking her (though that was regretted, and an accident); "calling her beggar, and reproaching her friends, which she took very stomachfully and reproached me justly with mine" (Feb. 28, 1665); "like a passionate fool" giving her "an evil name," for which he was afterward sorry (December 19, 1661); and now and then being provoked past silence by her spelling, her spending, her music, her following Court fashions.

She held her place. She gave back an evil name for his, and once told him he lied, and once, to pay his calling her a beggar, called him "pricklous"—a term sometimes hooted after a tailor. She rated him about Mrs. Knipp and Deb and the others, and when he was in bed she once came to him with red-hot tongs in a threat to pinch his nose. It was all very real and very trivial. They stand in these details like two children who are the best of friends, who quarrel, and who make it all up again. Always at the end, she did come to peace with him and he with her. He boggled mightily at giving her 20 pounds for an Easter dress, but he did give it and was pleased that she looked so handsome in the dress. The quarrels passed, and came again, and passed.

Scenes go on unendingly. Neither had learned to manage emotions. After they had been married five years (October 24, 1660), when he was twenty-seven and she nineteen, "I took occasion to be angry with my wife before I rose about her putting up of half a crown of mine in a paper box, which she had forgot where she had lain it. But we were friends again as we are always." In December, 1664, after they had been married nine years, being "very angry . . . for [her] not commanding her servants as she ought. . . . I did strike her over her left eye such a blow as the poor wretch did cry out and was in great pain, but yet her spirit was such as to endeavour to bite and scratch me. But I coying with her made her leave off crying, and sent for butter and parsley, and friends presently one with another, and I . . . vexed at my heart to think what I had done." After they had been married eleven years (December 7, 1666) he came "home to dinner, where finding the cloth laid and much crumpled but clean, I grew angry and flung the trenchers [dishes] about the room, and in a mighty heat I was: so a clean cloth was laid, and my poor wife very patient, and so to dinner." Then late in the evening "to supper, and mighty good friends with my poor wife." Six months after, "to the office all the afternoon . . . and then home in the evening, and there to sing and pipe with my wife, and that being done, she fell all of a sudden to discourse about her clothes and my humours in not suffering her wear them as she pleases, and grew to high words between us, but I fell to read a book (Boyle's Hydrostatiques) aloud . . . and let her talk, till she was tired and vexed that I would not hear her, and so [we] became friends" (June 4, 1667).

The episode of the white locks is long but clearly pointing. Pepys tells it this way: "This day my wife began to wear light-colored locks, quite white almost, which, though it makes her look very pretty, yet not being natural, vexes me, that I will not have her wear them" (March 13, 1665). A year and a half later, October 29, 1666, she is "mighty fine . . . with a new fair pair of locks, which vex me, though like a foole I helped her the other night to buy them." After seven months more of tension the explosion came. Pepys, late one evening as they drove home in a coach, "discovered my trouble to my wife for her white locks, swearing by God, several times, which I pray God forgive me for, and bending my fist, that I would not endure it." She "poor wretch, was surprised with it, and made me no answer all the way home; . . . there we parted, and I to the office late, and then home, and without supper to bed, vexed." The next morning, Sunday morning, she came to him while he was going over accounts, and after a round through calmness, anger, "very high terms," his talking

164

"like a severe foole," her crying, he gave her money to buy the
lace for her second mourning gown "and she promised to wear
no more white locks while I lived, and so all very good friends
as ever" by time for church (May 11, 12, 1667).

* * * * * *

There were other cross-currents and confusions. There was his
jealousy. Most men—Lord John Somerset's son home from France
or his own old bumbling Uncle Wight—were attracted to his wife.
Any man lay under suspicion of guilt and needed to be proved
innocent. Yet he knew that though she was gay and elusive and
sparkling and did not much like sour rules, she was steady in
weighing her moral conduct. "My old disease of jealousy," he
wrote in 1663.

Sharper than most was the jealousy which burned in him over
Mr. Pembleton, her dancing master, "a pretty neat black man"
(May 15, 1663). He was sure of his wife; yet even Lord Sandwich
had noticed she was beautiful; and Pembleton was a taking fellow.

Pembleton began teaching her on April 25, and the lessons
were to go on for a month. Soon the whole house was dancing.
Lessons came twice a day, "which," Pepys thought, "was a folly."
There was dancing before dinner and through the afternoon and
in the evening "till it was late"; Ashwell, his wife's companion,
took it up; friends joined in; and Pepys, convinced that dancing
"was a thing very useful for a gentleman," paid "entry money,"
10 shillings, and began lessons. By his oath he had to give half
as much to the poor. Within two days he wrote he would "be
able to do something with dancing ... in time." "They say that I
am like to make a dancer." At first he was not sure his wife would
ever dance well, but he came to think that after all she would
do it finely. That was in the first week of May.

Two days after the first lesson he feared "I have done very ill
in letting her learn to dance." Two weeks later he was "a little
angry with [his] wife for minding nothing now but the dancing-
master." Next, his "damned jealousy took fire" (May 19); he
watched. Sunday afternoon at St. Olave's, "over against our gallery
I espied Pembleton ... leer upon my wife all the sermon," and he
"observed she made a curtsey to him at coming out." An afternoon
that week when he went home he "found [them] and nobody else
in the house." He knew he should not spy, but he "laid [his] ear
to the door." He was sure of her but he had to prove his certainty
was truth. He did not find certainty by listening. He found only

165

"the deadly folly and plague that I bring upon myself to be so jealous" (May 29). The jealousy, he wrote, "do so trouble me that I know not at this very minute ... either [what] I write or am doing, nor how to carry myself to my wife. . . . I am grieved to the very heart." "This ... devilish jealousy ... makes a very hell in my mind, which the God of heaven remove ... So to the office" (May 26). He waited for the month to end.

When May was almost ended, the twenty-seventh, ". . . I waked by 3 o'clock, my mind being troubled ... and ... past 4 o'clock ... [as I was] going out of the bed [my wife] took hold of me and would know what ailed me." He told her. They had "an hour's discourse, sometimes high and sometimes kind ... and so after awhile I caressed her and parted ... friends, but she crying in a great discontent" (May 27). He was very busy all day, largely with Navy affairs—at the Temple, at St. James's, with the Chancellor of the Exchequer ("a very ready, quick, and diligent person"), and at Westminster Hall, "where Term and Parliament make the Hall full of" lawyers and M.Ps. "Thence by water to Chelsey, all the way reading a little book I bought of Improvement of Trade a pretty book and many things useful in it." At Chelsea he dined and heard music with Lord Sandwich, and afterward went into the Great Garden. He won a shilling from Lord Sandwich at nine-pins, and then "back as I came, to London Bridge, and so home." He found his wife "in a musty mood," ready to take offense and give it, for Pembleton had been there and she would not see him because her husband was away. Pepys told her to go dance with Pembleton when he came back; went to his office and worked; and was home before supper. Pembleton was there. Pepys and his wife danced together. She paid Pembleton, and "so he is cleared."

The day shows how busy Pepys usually was, and how important his business was, and how well he did it; and it shows how much alone Elizabeth Pepys was during a day. It shows, too, that though he carried all day the inextricable tangle of his jealousy, he did the business he set out to do. And it shows the interplay of his private emotions and his outside affairs. Almost every day, from different causes, he felt these alternations and conflicts.

They kept Pembleton to supper, and they all danced again. "I made myself ... kind to him as much as I could" (May 27). There it ended. Suspicion faded quite out. His wife seemed not to miss Mr. Pembleton or his lessons; yet two months later, in St. James's Park, "spying a man like Mr. Pembleton ... my blood did rise in my face and I fell into a sweat from my old jealousy and hate, which I pray God remove from me." Three or four months still later, in St. Olave's, Elizabeth Pepys pointed out Mr. Pembleton sitting with his wife, "a pretty little woman, well dressed, with a good jewel on her breast" (October 18, 1663). He may have seen them at church afterwards, but he noticed them for only two Sundays.

So the fire faded. In late October the jealousy had become "no great matter . . . which before was so terrible to me" (October 25). In December, "home to supper and to bed after some talke and Arithmetique with my poor wife, with whom now-a-days I live with great content, out of all trouble of mind by jealousy (for which God forgive me)." On December 31, 1664, he was sure, too sure it seems, that "a pretty and loving quiett family [he, his wife, and five or six servants] I have as any man in England." So, "Soon as ever the clock struck one, I kissed my wife in the kitchen by the fireside, wishing her a merry new yeare."

This tempest and whirlwind was like others of his—in its foolish start, its growing tension, its spying and self-disgust and suffering, its coming out so innocently to nothing in the end, and its being to Pepys after a while only "a far-off mountain fading into cloud."

* * * * * *

Pepys demanded the impossible from his wife. Of course he did not know how much he was asking. She was to stay the girl who had bemused him and translated him into happiness he had never imagined. She was to be always what she was when he was first in love with her, like the wind music at Massinger's play "when the angel comes down, which is so sweet that it ravished me, and . . . did wrap up my soul so that [I] remained all night transported" (February 27, 1668). With this, he expected her to be his wife, and a housekeeper, and a companion, and wise and encouraging. Besides, she was to retire into a cloud when he had work to do, and was to know without his telling when to leave him alone. She was, that is, to be all things to one man.

Unfortunately for his expectation, Elizabeth Pepys was strongly herself. She tried to be a good wife after his pattern, but she had to obey her own character and temperament and limits. She often was not well, and then Pepys was attentive and kindly affectionate. Her housekeeping at times went roughly. She did muddle the kitchen accounts, was slack or too strict in her oversight, suddenly was sure a maid was all bad and should be sent away off-hand; or what was worse, she gossiped with the maids, to Pepys's helpless distaste. She left her clothes about her room; she wore this or that in spite of her husband, though not for long; she wanted to follow Court styles of hairdressing, petticoats, and even of painting, and Pepys loathed paint on a woman's face as he did a grease-marked dish. She could not for long get on with most of his kin (Pepys hardly blamed her); and her singing was not always pure tone, as Knipp's was, nor her flageolet playing always true. She did not even dance superlatively—"a wave of the sea." Pepys knew women who did. When she lost her temper, she used "devil" to him, a word he profoundly disapproved of, and told her so, and she misnamed him and his family, and she complained of her loneliness and his neglect. He found she would be herself and not his patterned wife. When her moods were on her she did rasp him. She did not set the tune of her life to his words. She could not have done that however much she tried.

When Pepys first saw that his wife had stayed pretty much herself, he was bewildered. What he had laid down was proper and just, and clearly was best for them both. Then he was outraged by her tenacity, and her disrespect for him and her strange dullness. Then he was uneasy and most unhappy, as he was during the Pembleton episode. And then the whole relation settled into affection, with constant bickering over little things, and a few times with flares of anger that burned down close to the basis of their marriage.

So they went on through the Diary; each very individual; each complete, a substance of itself, yet both fused into the mystery of their union. He was strong-tempered, and in the earlier years of the Diary was not often tired ("to bed very weary, which I seldom am" April 11, 1662); very able and knowing it; intense in his opinions and purposes and emotion, and in the expression of them; quick-minded and quick-tempered; arrogant, prejudiced, sympathetic; sensitive, very nervous; judicious, affectionate; given to lapses, that took him low (with Deb, for instance) yet a moralist. She was different in character and blood; for fifteen years she had had different education and training, and had people around her of very different habit and standards and outlooks from his. She was French, from a haphazard home; and she had married an extraordinary man and was under the strain of living up to his success and his temperament.

Unity

Pepys saw no one equal to his wife, ever. For one thing, he was

168

sure she was beautiful. His certainty is all through the Diary, diffused; never shown by detail; never proved at all. It is induced by Pepys's sureness of it. He does not describe her—the color of her hair or of her eyes, her height, her voice, her way of walking, her gestures. He takes for granted the fact of her beauty as he takes the fact of London, and the sunrise, and himself. It never entered his mind that anyone would or could question it. He wrote that one of her portraits was beautiful. He did not write that she was beautiful. The compliment was to the painter for having caught a likeness to her beauty. Clearly, her beauty was a delight to him. When she was twenty, a friend at the Court took "my wife and I to the Queen's presence-chamber . . . and by and by the Queen [the mother of Charles II] and the two Princesses came to dinner." The Princess Henrietta Maria, then sixteen, was an admitted beauty. "The Princess . . . is very pretty. . . . But my wife standing near her . . . did seem to me much handsomer than she."

* * * * * *

Elizabeth Pepys was intelligent, though sometimes foolish. She was the only woman to whom Pepys told serious matters—his troubles while he was getting the Clerkship, his opinion of Sir William Penn, what he was planning for his father and his mother and Tom and Paulina, his letter to Lord Sandwich and his Great Speech before Parliament, the danger of anarchy in London when the Dutch were sailing up the Thames. With Mrs. Knipp, whom he admired very much and thought the best actress in London, he ate and danced and talked and visited behind the scenes, and he sang with her and, to his delight, heard her sing the songs he wrote. But that was the surface of a day, the gaiety of moving sunlight not the stability of his twenty-four hours. So, for Mrs. Pierce and others he liked to be with. Lady Castlemaine was faraway; her beauty shone on the edge of his romantic fancy.

Pepys was sure his wife had the accomplishments a lady should have. He regretted that her singing was not always true, yet he thought "it will come to something." She played the falgeolet and viol well enough for her pleasure and his, and danced with grace. She had learned backgammon from him (to Pepys, chess was a talked-about game played in Moscow during "the winter within doors") and some arithmetic and grammar while he had morning lessons. She recited French poems to him, and she read aloud well in English or French, and listened well when he read to her. She liked, as he did though less strongly, going to the theatre, the

169

pleasure of a party, the fun of "driving twice around Bartholemew fayer" in August, and of a Punch and Judy at a public park, and people, and some sorts of books, and always fine clothes and news of the Court, and a well-furnished home and a garden. She made quite perfect pastry. She had taste in buying and could bargain. She got on well enough if not over-well with his family and his colleagues in the Navy Office and their wives. "Her painting . . . I do love." Her "pictures . . . she is come to do finely . . . beyond what I could ever look for." He "admired [her] picture of our Saviour, now finished, which is very pretty" (September 27, 1665); "one fine woman's Persian head [was] mighty finely done" (August 5, 1665); and he was "mightily pleased with a Virgin's head that my wife is now doing of" (August 9, 1666). He showed her drawings, with his books and pictures, at his dinner for Lord Sandwich, Lord Peterboro, and the Ambassador to Spain.

A certainty the Diary tells, is his need of her. He did not ever write that straight out; he took it as accepted, as he did any acknowledged truth. She was part of his life and of him, in the way his work was and music and a few other things. It is typical and pleasant, and a little amusing, that when he had to learn the multiplication table for his Clerkship, he taught it to her; and when he was learning the flageolet or the viol or had written a song, she was to learn it, too; and when he had his portrait painted, he had hers painted. Both of them seem to have enjoyed their common employments.

He rested in her affection. He "was grieved in [his] heart" to have her away from him, "being worse by much without her" (July 5, 1665). He liked to be with her on ordinary days; and when he was troubled or was very happy. They walked together in the garden of the Navy Office, evening, and in the fields outside Bow near Bethnal Green. They went up the river to Vauxhall, and to the shows at Bartolemy Fair, and Sundays to St. Olave's. He was happy at home with her—reading, talking, singing, eating his meals. When she was not well he had dinner beside her bed, "in great content" that he was near her. She encouraged him in the time he was getting his appointment as Clerk of the Acts. The afternoon he was sure he had the Clerkship, he brought her to the City by coach and presented to her, with a gesture, his Royal Patent.

He worried when she was at Dulwich during the Plague, though he had a good time alone. When she was away, he looked forward to her letters and to being with her again. At the end of one tire-

170

some day in May, 1667, he wrote: "late at my office at business, and so home to supper and sing a little with my dear wife."

In the early spring of 1668, Parliament, a long time at odds with the Navy Office, summoned its Principal Officers to defend themselves before the bar of the House. Pepys was chosen to speak for the Navy. He had four days to prepare. The night before he was to speak, he went to bed tired out and depressed and discouraged —"quite weary, and dull, and vexed"—by the "muchness of the business," "the task I have upon me," "what the issue of it may be." Thursday, the day of his Great Speech, his entry begins: "5th. With these thoughts I lay troubling myself till six o'clock, restless, and at last getting my wife to talk to me to comfort me, which she at last did. . . . So with great trouble, but yet with some ease, from this discourse with my wife, I up . . . and by nine o'clock . . . W. [Hewer] with me to Westminster," where Pepys talked three hours before Parliament with great success for the Navy and with very great and deserved satisfaction to himself. The day's long entry ends "home . . . and there to my wife, whom W. Hewer had told my success, and she overjoyed . . .; and, after talking awhile . . . to bed, having had no quiet rest a good while."

Pepys was more open with his wife than with anyone else. He spoke almost as openly to her as he wrote in the Diary—almost, for some uneasy matters he did not talk of. He wrote of them. The Diary merely received. It was his passive companion. He expected nothing back from it. From Elizabeth Pepys he expected response, agreement, encouragement, sympathy, comfort. He expected warmth. She gave it to him almost always; always, it seems, for important and honest matters and usually for his prejudices and whims and vagaries of mood. To his bewilderment, she sometimes disagreed over small matters of talk, dress, spending, servants, or his brother Tom and his sister Paulina, and going to his father's for months; and she disagreed with energy over conduct of his he knew was wrong. The small disagreements were likely to make him more impatient than the large. The large, grieved and troubled him. Perhaps, because a large disagreement was serious, he took it up with less hurry and irritation, looked at it more steadily, felt it more deeply, and in the end spoke and acted more fairly.

He was certain he was wiser than his wife and should rule in the house. This conviction was deep in his character and strong in the time. He was by nature arrogant; usually charming in it, seldom high-handed, yet arrogant. His wife especially, he was convinced, needed his direction. She gave up to caprices of temper, to the excitement of her imagination and of what he thought were small matters. Then their house became most uncomfortable. He thought she was best when she was with him, for so she caught his mood and took his interests. He wrote of her "neglect of things" when he was not with her, of "her impertinent humours got by this liberty of being from me, which she is never to be trusted with" (June 17, 1668), of her getting sudden dislikes and unfounded prejudices, of her having after a visit "something in her gizzard that only waits an opportunity of being provoked to bring up." He knew that what he did sometimes upset her, that he demanded a great deal from her, and that being for two months with his old parents —the imperfect wife of their perfect son—stretched her nerves beyond judiciousness. He knew, too, "the unquiet life . . . my mother makes my father . . . live through her want of reason." Yet once when his wife came home from them, her temper jangled, he wrote "she is a fool" (June 17, 1668).

Yet Pepys understood her better, saw more her purposes and cross-purposes, her impulses pleasant and sharp, and gave her more sympathy than usually he is credited with. He came to know that she must largely have her own life, that much of her time she spent away from him, and that her days began as early as his and were long and often empty (she "do live very lonely"), and that though she had many acquaintances she had no family worth counting, and no deep friend but him. He knew he was faulty toward her: "My wife this night [was] troubled at my leaving her alone so much and keeping her within doors, which indeed I do not well nor wisely in" (April 28, 1667). Unfortunately, he did not tell her his understanding, his sense of mistake, his affection and concern for her happiness. He was busy, and he never liked to admit he was wrong, and he seems to have thought such admissions would make his influence less. He was sure—first and last—she needed his directing. He was sure she was best when she was with him and he, tacitly or in words, was shaping her acts and feelings; shaping them, that is, as far as he could, for he realized she had strength and resilience and the aloofness of youth. A young tree must grow, if at all, in its own nature. Unfortunately, too, by his openness with her he showed her the worst in himself—intense turns of temper, unreason and prejudice, tension and the accumulated hidden pressure of the day. He had less restraint before her than before anyone else.

Her dependence on him he realized but not enough to be always patient and tactful. He loved her, but once not being in a mood of

172

wisdom, when he heard her "sing now and then a note out of tune" as he was singing with her, he could "not bear with that in her which is fit I should." Afterwards he was troubled that he had showed his impatience and wrote: "I do find that I do put her out of heart, and make her fearful to sing before me" (October 30, 1666). Just as his impatience and her singing made her sing badly, so his starting a quarrel brought on her counter-quarrel. When she told him she wanted a woman to be with her as a companion, "Before and after we were in bed we had much talk and difference between us about . . . having a woman." The next day they were "up and began our discontent again." Yet in the end he did agree. It is typical that he did not tell her why he gave in to what she wanted.

Five quotations show part of what he felt, deeply.

"To the office, and sat there all the afternoon till 9 at night. So home to my musique, and my wife and I sat singing in my chamber a great while together, and then to bed" (May 17, 1661).

"I home and heare my boy play on the lute, and [took] a turn with my wife pleasantly in the garden by moonshine, my heart being in great peace" (March 7, 1666).

"This day, by the blessing of God, my wife and I have been married nine years: but my head being full of business, I did not think of it to keep it in any extraordinary manner. But bless God for our long lives and loves and health together, which the same God long continue, I wish, from my very heart!" (October 10, 1664.)

"So home to my wife, whom I find not well, in bed, and it seems hath not been well these two days. She rose and we to dinner, after dinner up to my chamber, where she entertained me with what she hath lately bought of clothes for herself, and Demask linnen, and other things for the house. I did give her a serious account how matters stand with me, of favour with the King and Duke, and of danger in reference to my Lord's and Sir G. Carteret's falls, and the dissatisfaction I have heard the Duke of Albermarle hath acknowledged to somebody, among other things, against my Lord Sandwich, that he did bring me into the Navy against his desire and endeavour for another, which was our doting foole Turner. Thence from one discourse to another, and looking over my house, and other things I spent the day at home" (January 30, 1666).

"Lay long in bed, talking with pleasure with my poor wife, how she used to make coal fires, and wash my foul clothes with her own hand for me, poor wretch! in our little room at my Lord Sandwich's [before they had even the house in Axe Yard]; for which I ought for ever to love and admire her, and do; and persuade myself she would do the same thing again, if God should reduce us to it" (February 25, 1667).

Pepys then was wealthy, with 8,000 pounds to his credit and a good income and a fine house.

All of the Diary shows that Pepys thought no one equal to his wife, ever; and it shows that she kept on and on disturbing him by not following the ways he marked out for her acts and opinions and moods. It shows, too, most certainly, that to him the second was nothing beside the first.

ENVOY

The Diary is a small part of what Pepys wrote and it is different from the rest. He kept it for himself. It is an intimate, hidden monologue, written frankly and swiftly to get down what had stirred his mind each day. That a mood, an opinion, the memory of an action or of an impulse stayed in his mind made it worth recording. He did not expect his diary to be read in his life, if it ever was read. It was to lie below the horizon of his time; and to make more sure it should not be seen by anyone named in it or left unnamed, he put it in the safe obscurity of cipher. He never polished what he had written after it was in the Diary, and he may never have reread it.

Today the Diary lies open and so, it seems, does Pepys's life. Not all of it. The Diary is an intimate record and a true one, but incomplete. For one thing, it covers nine and a half years out of seventy; and, for another, Pepys could not tell the absolute truth about himself because he could not know himself absolutely. And the Diary covers a time of constant change. When the Diary began the Commonwealth was ending. Pepys and the rest of England were under the tension of uncertainty and danger. Pepys was young, about twenty-seven, and his wife was eighteen, and both were immature. His position, too, was changing. Just before the Diary began they were living in a "garret," on a pound a week, and seeing ahead a disturbingly clouded future; in two years, he gained social standing, a secure future, and a satisfying income.

His years as Clerk of the Acts were crowded for him and amazing. Time rushed by. It vibrated with his pleasant and alarming discoveries about himself and others; with puzzling adjustments, plans and hopes and opinions, and blunders and success; with many people, of all sorts; with the Plague and the Great Fire; secret impatience at himself but more often with others, and dissatisfactions over matters in general; with triumphs at the Navy Office and in society; with pride in having a good house

175

beautifully furnished and a good income, a garden, and a coach;, with new knowledge and newly-realized abilities; and with the old round of temptations and lapses and regrets. The Diary tells these. It is a succession of new sunrises. It records nine and a half years in London, from January 1, 1660 to June 1, 1669. It shows how stirring and difficult, and, in the end, good, the rush of his life seemed to him. It gives his character and temperament and action as a young man, and points up strong qualities in him, and suggests by his emphasis something of what, possibly and perhaps (who knew?), he might become. The Diary could not show and did not guess at the certainties after 1669, as it sometimes is pressed to do.

* * * * * *

A biography, long or short, covers a limited time, and even of that time there is much it has not knowledge or space or wish to tell. It is a limited portrait. Like a portrait it can put down only part of a life, whether it tells ten days or fifty years, and it can put down only what the painter sees. A painter is held to his own powers and to an instant of time. Yet if he is a good painter he shows the current which through many years controls the shifting flow of many thoughts and moods and acts. The painter can give the constant truth. He can catch a flash in time that holds the long extent. He paints the turn of the head, the suddenly arrested look, the momentary and unforgettable light on face and clothing, on colors and forms, and the transient and fitting background of architecture or landscape. Yet by these passing details he shows what is lasting. Though a biography tells of many years, it, too, is limited, yet it can catch some, or much, that lasts.

The Diary is inspired biography. It is the best self-portrait written in English. Within its brevity and the limit of its substance, it tells a hundred thousand details and gathers them into a point of light, a unity compounded of many diversities. The Diary is an inspired biography but Pepys wrote it. Inspiration in each man it touches works out a unique result. Genius displayed—the only way we know it—is always individual. However strong genius is, it is bounded by what embodies it. Pepys's voice tells what is told. The Diary gives out the warmth of his experience; it brings exactly the climate of his nature at home and in his office and abroad in London. Power to give such reality is genius. Yet there is much the Diary does not do and, it seems, could not do and never thought of doing; and there is danger of overlooking what Pepys does not have and even of praising the lack.

176

The Diary makes clear that Pepys's emotions were constantly alive, many of them intense or at least out of proportion to their causes, and others touching him only enough to draw in his lips with passing impatience, or riffle the surface of an entry with irritation or light pleasure. His feelings were quick-changing, constant, intense, and not always under his judgment or his purpose. Sometimes he raised a feeling to a certainty. Yet the open play of feeling gives the Diary much of its color.

Then, in contradiction to emotion, he had cool good sense, a steadied and level mind, which at times toughened into cynical rejection of "enthusiasm" and nonsense. His nature was surprisingly hard. He could analyze coolly a question, outline action, build a telling brief; and his business letters and agenda were to the point and led step-by-step clearly to the point. His mind was practical, tenacious, adroit, logical, intensely observant, and strong. He saw what was needed and the way to it. He judged shrewdly his antagonists and his obstacles. That is, he was all this until his feelings mixed into the matter; then farewell judgment, logic, the cool mind.

Pepys was inherently a moralist. Rather, he was what, if he had defined, he might have thought all moralists were—a rational man; and it must be added that he was a practical rationalist, not a philosopher. His beliefs were those he judged good and possible for men to carry out, even though he knew he himself could not always follow them. What he accepted was laid down in the Bible, if seldom in detail; and from the Bible and from their own lives, honourable and able men with knowledge and experience of the world, during many years, had derived a code of duties—to one's family and kin and friends, to society and England and the Church, in business and in amusements, in intimate or large matters, in a time of trouble or of happiness.

Now and then, an idea or a feeling or an action which especially caught Pepys's interest (a sense impression—except music—seldom did) had for him the freshness of something newly-created. He gave it, as a child might have, all the energy of his attention. He found himself alone with it, other things shut out. The wind-music of *The Virgin Martyr*, which he heard one afternoon in 1668, was "so sweet that . . . going home, and at home," and "all night" he "remained . . . transported." His duty to build a great Navy grew more certain with time, Lady Castlemaine more a delight to look at, Sir W. Penn or another colleague less to be borne, a dish marked by greasy fingers more "sluttish," his own success more dazzling and sure—than any of them would have been to another man.

177

Usually a wonder drained away or another wonder cut it short; but sometimes one recurred and increased, as his feeling for his wife did, and his certainty that he should see to England's Navy. This freshness—eager, possessive, high-keyed, and individual—is a normal feeling and a fairly common one, though not in the degree or with the constancy Pepys felt it. From their own memories, most readers of the Diary know that Pepys is telling what is true.

Things of the spirit—assurances or questions—do not touch the Diary. Pepys found the forms of earth enough. What was close to him, what he did every day at work and at home and in his leisure, what speculations they led to, satisfied him fully. The Diary makes these interests vivid, often dazzling; yet Pepys never implied that beyond his interests might exist wonders unseen and not to be guessed.

The Diary does not hold realities of the spirit—profound humanity, the strength and comfort of faith, the serenity of beauty. It lacks even a dim sense that there is a mystery of *here, you,* and the intense *I*. Pepys might well have found such a sentence only high words.

Some qualities of a great book, the Diary does not have. Pepys has made his own book, which in its way is close to perfect. It is unique, constantly fresh, true in the changes of three hundred years, and—what most gives it its value—it creates life by its words. The Diary is an inspired biography; it is, admirably, what it is; and for other things the reader may read another book.

SAMUEL PEPYS IN THE DIARY
has been printed in Linotype Caledonia
on White Saturn Book
by William G. Johnston Company
and bound in Interlaken Black Cloth
by S. A. Stewart Company
for the University of Pittsburgh Press
in the *Year of the Pittsburgh Bicentennial.*